WI

RAISING EMOTIONALLY HEALTHY BOYS

Other books by Michael Reist

The Dysfunctional School
Raising Boys in a New Kind of World
What Every Parent Should Know About School

RAISING
EMOTIONALLY
HEALTHY
BOYS

MICHAEL REIST

DUNDURN
TORONTO

The stories of individuals contained in this book are based upon real events; however, names and other details have been changed to protect their privacy. Any similarities between these stories and individuals known to the reader are purely coincidental.

Project Editor: Jennifer McKnight
Copy Editor: Jess Shulman
Design: Laura Boyle
Cover Design: Laura Boyle
Cover Image: Fancy Photography / Veer
Printer: Webcom

Library and Archives Canada Cataloguing in Publication

Reist, Michael, author
        Raising emotionally healthy boys / Michael Reist.

Includes bibliographical references and index. Issued in print and electronic formats.
ISBN 978-1-4597-3139-4 (bound).--ISBN 978-1-4597-3140-0 (pdf).-- ISBN 978-1-4597-3141-7 (epub)

1. Boys. 2. Parenting. 3. Child rearing. 4. Child psychology. I. Title.

HQ775.R457 2015   649'.132   C2015-900567-1
                                   C2015-900568-X

1   2   3   4   5   19   18   17   16   15

  Conseil des Arts   Canada Council
                      du Canada   for the Arts

Canada

 ONTARIO ARTS COUNCIL
                      CONSEIL DES ARTS DE L'ONTARI
                      an Ontario government agency
                      un organisme du gouvernement de l'Ontar

We acknowledge the support of the **Canada Council for the Arts** and the **Ontario Arts Council** for our publishing program. We also acknowledge the financial support of the **Government of Canada** through the **Canada Book Fund** and **Livres Canada Books**, and the **Government of Ontario** through the **Ontario Book Publishing Tax Credit** and the **Ontario Media Development Corporation**.

Care has been taken to trace the ownership of copyright material used in this book. The author and the publisher welcome any information enabling them to rectify any references or credits in subsequent editions.

— *J. Kirk Howard, President*

Printed and bound in Canada.

VISIT US AT
Dundurn.com | @dundurnpress | Facebook.com/dundurnpress | Pinterest.com/dundurnpress

Dundurn
3 Church Street, Suite 500
Toronto, Ontario, Canada
M5E 1M2

This book is dedicated to the memory of
Cecilia Kennedy
Poet, teacher, friend

Contents

"I've always felt like an imposter. It's a particularly male problem. Most males live in some kind of dread of being found out."
— Comedian Stephen Fry

"He didn't even want me to take them in my arms when they were crying. He just forbid me. He was saying that they would be spoiled."
— Monique Lépine, mother of Marc Lépine, perpetrator of the Montreal Massacre, speaking about Marc's father

"The most political thing you can do is be yourself."
— George O'Dowd (Boy George)

"All wars are civil wars — men against their brothers."
— James Hollis

"Peer power grows as mentoring diminishes."
— Eugene Monick

What Is Emotional Health?

One cannot have a healthy or an unhealthy emotion. Our emotions cannot be sick. Emotions are completely natural and arise from the conditions in which we find ourselves. They are like the weather. Storms come and go, clouds form and disperse, fog rolls in, the sun shines brightly. Weather is not good or bad. It is neutral. When we talk about bad weather and good weather, we are talking about the judgments we are passing on it, and these judgments always have to do with how the weather is hindering or helping us. Feelings are the same. They come and go according to certain "systems." The difference between weather systems and emotional systems is that we create or at least have some control over the conditions that create these feelings. Likewise, as we can decide how to respond to the weather, we can decide how to respond to our feelings.

An emotionally healthy person is someone who does not block their feelings, but *has* their feelings. It has been said that if you don't have your feelings, your feelings will have you. Psychologists use the word *repression* for what we do to our feelings. We press them down. When we press anything down, it doesn't go away. It intensifies. Think of water or air under pressure. It will not be contained. It must get out. If it can't get out in natural ways, it will get out in other ways. Our feelings are the same. They must get out. We must learn to *have* our feelings. Not just because of the damage that repressing them will cause but also because of the pleasure we miss. Incredibly, we repress pleasurable feelings as well as unpleasurable ones. The mechanism of repression becomes so ingrained that we shut down, repress, and stifle all emotions. The emotionally healthy person is the one in whom the emotions flow like water. The image of the flowing stream is a good one for understanding our emotions. Water goes where it will. When we dam the stream, the land (our consciousness) becomes flooded. The same thing happens when we dam our feelings. The river overflows its banks and what started out as an innocent flow becomes something destructive and problematic.

When I talk about raising emotionally healthy boys, I am not talking about what we need to do *to* them. I am talking about what we must *avoid* doing. Children are born with powerful, healthy, fully functioning emotional lives. Why then does the happy, spontaneous child develop into an angry, depressed teenager? Sometimes the answer lies in chemistry, but more often the answer lies in the environment in which he finds himself. This environment includes all the people who clip, trim, water, and fertilize this young plant. Some boys grow up to be flourishing, fully-functioning adults. Others grow up to be emotionally stunted versions of what they could have been. Why does this happen? I am not talking about raising the perfect child. I'm talking about raising boys to achieve as much of their inner potential as possible. This is a book about the future, about the adults we are raising right now. The future needs our boys to be healthy, whole, and strong, so that as adults they can help to create a better world than the one we have left to them.

How Do Feelings Work?

Our emotions are strongly connected to our thoughts. What we think influences how we feel. One person will look at a situation, think about it, and feel excited or happy. Another person will look at the same situation, think about it, and feel nervous or sad. When Mary found out she was pregnant, she went into a depression, thinking about her own sad childhood and all the problems in the world today. When Anne found out she was pregnant, she was overjoyed at the prospect of all the positive experiences that lay ahead. What causes such differences in the ways people think about their experiences? One cause is our own past experience and how it has shaped our thinking; the other cause is how we have been taught to think about certain things. In order to be effective, positive parents, we must reflect on the experiences that shaped our thinking as well as the attitudes we were taught. Parenting can be about reproducing old patterns or it can be an incredible opportunity to try out new ways of being. What we do influences what we think, so when we try out new ways, we end up thinking in new ways. What has been done to us influences how we think and act, but this is not the end of the story. We can choose how to think and act, and this book tries to present alternative options regarding how we might think about boys and how we might act with boys because how we think about them and how we act with them will influence how they think and act in the future.

The Attitudes We Bring to Parenting

The mother who sees her child as a problem to be solved or an obstacle to be overcome is going to parent very differently from a parent who sees her child as a gift to be unpacked or a mystery to be discovered. Parents with a negative defeatist attitude have said to me, "I don't *want* to feel this way." Our feelings spring from our innate nature or temperament. A highly sensitive, highly reactive parent who thrives on predictability and structure will deal with a newborn very differently than a parent who is more comfortable with disorder. One of the most important things we must do as parents is to understand our own temperament, our own nature. We need to anticipate and manage how we deal with certain situations. Because we deal with things differently from others doesn't make our response wrong. We only need to ensure that we understand and respect the child's nature at the same time. Parenting then becomes a negotiation or compromise between our own needs and those of the child. There will be some ways in which we can change our thinking and behaviour and other ways in which we cannot. That's just the way we're made. But many parents will opt for their default mode not because they can't change, but because it's just easier not to. "The child is the one who has to change, not me." This is the kind of challenge I want to present in this book. Let's honour our own nature. Let's honour the nature of our children.

So much of our stress as parents results from our expectations. "I expect myself to be a perfect parent. I expect that I should never have any problems. I expect that all other parents are doing a better job than I am." If we expect perfection and don't get it, we judge ourselves harshly. If we don't expect perfection and do get something positive, we think of it as luck. We don't enjoy it and take pride in it. The concepts of *automatic negative thoughts* and *cognitive distortions* (which have roots in cognitive behavioural therapy) have a lot of relevance for parents. When we fall into automatic negative thinking, our kids are learning something. They will pick up our attitude. Boys are a problem. Girls are a problem. Life is hard. The world is going to the dogs. The list goes on. Cognitive distortions occur when we twist our thinking to make events fit our view of the world. We think our child is lazy, yet he does well on a test — the teacher must be an easy marker, it must have been an easy test, it's the one subject he's good at. We make the world fit our image of it. In this book I will deal with many core beliefs about boys that we carry around as individuals but also as a culture. I will also challenge some of the cognitive distortions that we all engage in to make boys fit our image of them.

Emotional Health Starts with Mom and Dad

If we want to take our children somewhere, emotionally, we have to go there first or go there with them. We cannot send them into emotional health while we remain stuck. This is the great opportunity and the great challenge of parenting — to change ourselves. Many parents bring their kids to me to be "fixed," but often the parents need to do some fixing themselves. The mental and emotional health of children depends very much on their environment. Children absorb the emotional tone of the household; they are intimately affected by Mom and Dad's emotional health. If we want our kids to be happy, we have to get happy ourselves. If we want our kids to have strong self-esteem, then we have to work on our own. For our kids to be healthy, whole, and strong, they must have role models very close to them who are healthy, whole, and strong. These are not things we can preach or teach or train into a child. They must be part of the environment and the culture of the home. It seems like a daunting task, because we immediately think this means we have to be perfect parents. This is not what it means. What it means is that we are parents on a path or in a process. We are constantly questioning, learning, and growing. A good parent is a conscious parent; they think about what they do, and they ask themselves how they could do things better. They think about their own family of origin, their own upbringing. They ask themselves what they want to keep and what they want to let go of. Conscious parents don't just work on their children; they work on themselves. They want to become better people. They try to become the kind of parents they want their children to have. Parenting happens over many years. Through all our children's developmental stages, we need to show them that to live is to change and grow and come to greater awareness. I feel sad when I meet parents who have stopped growing, who are not interested in changing themselves — only in changing their children. They say, "I am what I am. I know what I know. I'm doing the best I can." At the other end of the spectrum is the parent who over-analyzes and over-thinks every tiny decision. This is not healthy either, and it is often motivated by anxiety and fear, the fear that "I'm a bad parent and I'm going to screw up my kids." We have to find a middle ground, one with a positive, open-ended, confident approach, and above all, we have to have a sense of humour. The great gift of parenting is that we get to work on ourselves. We begin by thinking we need to know everything about parenting and that we can turn our children into whatever we want them to be. We end up discovering that our children already have an inner imperative that we do not create but witness. Our children can teach us a tremendous amount. This book is meant to guide us to and through those lessons.

What Kind of Men Do We Want Our Boys to Be?

For years we have talked about empowering girls to become strong women by rejecting traditional gender roles and pursuing their own interests, developing their innate abilities, and participating fully in a man's world. Now the same effort has to be put into boys. We need to empower our boys to transcend the restrictive sex roles they have been thrust into. Like girls, they need to be permitted to embrace a broader range of interests and behaviour — to fully participate in "a woman's world" — a world where emotions are allowed and nurturing behaviour is expected. When talking about the emotional health of boys, we need to start with a vision of what kind of men we want our boys to become. We want men who are strong, confident, and whole in the best sense of these words.

The Strong Man

In our culture, strength has come to be associated with power over others and is often too closely aligned with violence. This has got to change. The strong man is the man of focus, commitment, determination, and self-discipline. The strong man has the courage to do what needs to be done, to say what needs to be said. The strong man plays a vital role in his community, and sometimes that means critiquing his community when he thinks it is going in the wrong direction. The strong man stands firm in his convictions. He fights for what is right and true. He protects those in his care.

The Confident Man

Confidence comes from having a world view, a vision, an overriding goal or orientation in one's life. A confident man knows what he stands for and what he believes in, and he lives his life according to those beliefs. He makes every choice in light of this vision. Confidence does not mean arrogance or self-righteousness. In popular culture, we have too many images of a confident man who listens to no one; he is always right and condemns those views that are different from his own. But the truly confident man has humility. He holds onto his truth, but is always open to growth, change, and learning. He does not feel threatened by those who see the world differently. He is not just confident in what he is; he is confident in what he is going to become, and he is confident about making the decisions that will take him there.

The Whole Man

So many men are broken and fragmented. They have neglected or rejected huge parts of themselves — their intellect, their emotions, their spirituality, their bodies. They become money-making machines, buying machines, sex machines, power and control machines. The whole man uses his intelligence for analytical and critical thought. Using analytical thought he asks, "Why is this happening?" Using critical thought he asks, "Should this be happening? Is it good or bad, right or wrong?" This intelligent thought becomes the basis for action in one's life. The whole man is willing to get up off the couch and do something.

The issue of emotional repression is a particular issue for males. Boys are socialized from a very young age to hide their emotions. Girls, on the other hand, are allowed a much broader range of emotional expression. The long-term repercussions of this are profound. The whole man is someone who is allowed and allows himself the whole spectrum of emotional life. He is open to the emotions of others. He thinks of emotions in a positive way. He knows that they animate people and make them loveable. He is open to the light end of the emotional spectrum as well as the dark end. He can laugh and cry. He can feel joy as well as anger. He is capable of intimacy — with women, children, and other men.

The whole man acknowledges his own spiritual dimension and the spiritual dimension of reality. He acknowledges that science, technology, and reason may not explain everything. He has the spiritual awareness to throw up his hands in awe at the wonder of nature and the universe, to see it as something mysterious and profound — something to be respected, not exploited for material gain.

The whole man lives in his body. He does not deny his body. How many men refuse to see a doctor, or only go when there is a glaring problem? In popular culture, men are often depicted as being interested only in their muscles, their stomachs, and their genitals. This is what the body has been reduced to. The whole man takes care of his body through diet, exercise, and sleep. The whole man who is comfortable with his own body becomes comfortable with the bodies of others. As he stops treating his own body as an object to be controlled, he stops seeing other bodies the same way. The whole man is a sensual man. He can take pleasure in all five senses. As he becomes comfortable with his sensual self, he is able to meet the sensual needs of others — especially those he loves and who love him.

Raise Emotionally Healthy Boys and Change the World

The central thesis of this book is that if we raised emotionally health-ier boys, the world would be a significantly better place. Many of the problems we face as a society and as a species are directly influenced by the way we raise our boys. The growing gap between rich and poor, the destruction of the environment, street violence and war, the subju-gation and abuse of women — all of these phenomena have significant roots in the male psyche and male culture. The source of the problem is not found in the intrinsic biological nature of males. It is to be found in the way males are shaped and formed by the cultures and institutions they grow up in. We are all products of nature and nurture combined. Sometimes our nurturing enhances our nature; sometimes it degrades it. This is what we need to talk about. As we come to the end of four to five thousand years of patriarchy, we are faced with the need to re-define masculinity. This is a great opportunity for growth, renewal, and liberation. Our boys are lucky to be living in such a time, and they are even luckier when they have adults in their lives who are open to considering new ways of being male and female. They are lucky when they have adults in their lives who are aware of how boys function and of what they need.

Emotionally damaged boys grow up to be our criminals, our abusers of women and children. They grow up to be our addicts, our warmongers, our environment destroyers. They grow up to be our power-junkies, our Wall Street greed demons, our purveyors of con-scienceless capitalism that leads to poverty alongside gross consump-tion. These men are *our* criminals, abusers, etc. because the respons-ibility for these things does not lie just with the individual, nor does it lie only with men — as though there was something inherently wrong with them. The responsibility for the way some boys grow up to be de-structive men lies with all of us.

Perhaps the biggest factor influencing gender roles is our cultural inheritance called patriarchy. (The term comes from the Greek word *patriarkhia* meaning *rule by the father* but more broadly understood as *rule by men*). In the West, patriarchy is slowly crumbling, but it still persists as the dominant social paradigm. Politics, business, religion, education, and the family itself are all based on a patriarchal model: top-down power and control, authoritarianism, competition, repression of emotion, conformity. The most important thing to say about patriarchy is that it is not a conscious conspiracy on the part of men to "rule the world." Patriarchy is a social system rooted in a deep psychic fear — fear of the loss of power and control. Men are as much the victims of patriarchy as women are. Ironically, patriarchy is not only sustained by those for whom it works (the Vladimir Putins and Donald Trumps) but also by those for whom it doesn't work!

Feminism has had such a hard ride because it is the first social movement to seriously threaten patriarchy. It is the inevitable antidote that we need. The frustrating thing about feminism is that it has often held up the patriarchal yardstick of success for women — "you too can now sacrifice yourself on the altar of power, status, money, and possessions." Men eventually agreed to let women in on the game on the condition that the game itself not be changed. Feminists hoped that women would enter patriarchal structures and change them, but this has not happened — yet. They have adapted themselves to the old boys club in order to gain entry. As a result, the multinational corporation implicated in environmental destruction or human rights abuses continues to operate unchallenged under the female CEO.

One of the keys that might unlock the grip of patriarchy is emotions. To the extent that men are divorced from how they feel, they accept bizarre and damaging life situations. Women are emotionally healthier than men because they are permitted a broader range of emotional response to their lives. Men are trained to have a muted response to their own lives. They learn this lesson so well that even when situations are intolerable, they press on in silence. In 1854 Henry David Thoreau wrote, "The mass of men lead lives of quiet desperation." He wrote this in a time we think of as an idyllic, rural, innocent past in North America. What would he say about the millions of commuters who pour into office towers each morning and pour out again to the suburbs each night? For this system to continue, emotional life must be denied. Men know this and, ironically, feel this. Perhaps people are driven to action more by feelings than by thoughts. Men have yet to harness this energy. Men have the same feelings women do. They have just learned to suppress, ignore, rationalize, and medicate those feelings until they become transformed into other things. When men become emotionally healthy, social change will be more possible.

The final thing men and boys will need is leadership. When what it means to be a woman changed, women and girls had a whole cultural movement behind them, coaching them along the way. Men have been left to figure out on their own how to deal with this sea change in Western society. They have no social movement coaching them through it. They are making it up as they go along, and the general result has been confusion and sometimes anger. One of the reasons some men are hostile to feminism is envy. The unspoken cry behind their criticism is "what about me? What about what I want?" It's a legitimate question that has never been answered. Women have gained greater freedom, autonomy, happiness, and fulfillment. Men want the same things. They just don't know how to get them. We need a social movement that will redefine masculinity. We begin this project by changing the way we raise boys.

Part 1
Parenting Boys

Boys need what all children need, but it is important to see these needs through a particular lens. Because boys are biologically different from girls and because they are socialized differently, their needs have to be seen in this context. Boys are the product of both nature and nurture. We serve our boys better when we understand their inherent nature (their biology and their chemistry) and when we look at the way we nurture them. We need to work with their inherent nature (over which we have no control) and make new decisions about the best ways to nurture them (something we can control). Men and boys are the product of millions of years of evolution, but they are also the product of the cultures that raise them in the present. As I have said, our cultural inheritance of patriarchy is obsolete, and we are in the process of creating a new culture in which gender roles and gender identity are undergoing profound changes. Let's look at what needs to be kept and what needs to be changed if we are going to raise emotionally healthy boys.

1

Seeing Ourselves in Our Children

Sometimes we do not see our children for who they really are because we see them through the lens of our own self-perceptions. We will be able to love and accept our children more fully when we learn to love and accept ourselves. We bring many unresolved issues to our parenting that originated for the most part in our own childhood. We felt awkward as a child, so we tense up when our child appears awkward. We lived under many constraints with strict parents, so we feel resentful when our child demonstrates behaviour that is free and spontaneous. We felt stupid in school, so we are determined that our child will not be stupid. We were not popular in school, so our child must be popular. The list of childhood issues like this could go on. The issues are different for everyone, but we need to look at them. When parents come to me concerned about their child's performance in school, I often ask them about their own experience in school. Many times the parent's anxiety is rooted in themselves, not the child. They are afraid of the child experiencing the same thing they did, or more precisely they are afraid of experiencing their own trauma again through their child. Their concern is rooted in a deep love for the child, but it is also rooted in a deep need for self-protection.

Bill, a man in his fifties, was raised by a stern, distant, critical father. He had been a spontaneous, joyful, creative child, but his spirit was crushed by his father's condemning words and actions. In middle age, Bill went through a deep depression. When his own son was ten years old he demonstrated many of the characteristics Bill had at that age. One of these characteristics was talking incessantly — not silly, frenetic talk but enthusiastic, intelligent talk that sprang from a passion for life. Bill would literally wince when his son talked. I asked Bill about this, and he admitted that his son's behaviour drove him crazy. He could see himself in his son, who was exhibiting exactly the kind of behaviour that his peers and his father used to mock. A young boy who talks freely and enthusiastically in his high-pitched voice can attract bullies who latch onto this and ridicule him with words like *fag* and *gay*, trying to extinguish his expressiveness. They can shame a child into denying his true nature. The self-talk of the happy, carefree child is "I love who I am." When his nature is repeatedly mocked and rejected, his self-talk becomes toxic: "I hate who I am." This is one of the greatest tragedies that can happen to a child, yet if we are really honest with ourselves, this has happened to all of us on some level. What makes it even more disturbing is when it is done by the child's parents. Bill said that when he listens to his son, his main thought is "why can't you be different?" This is a message that plays in many people's heads. It's the companion of other messages, such as "you're not good enough," "there's something wrong with you," or "you don't measure up." We feel it about ourselves. We project it onto our children. They pick it up. Bill saw his own gifts as weaknesses to be purged. His father refused to see and accept his son's true nature, and now Bill was doing the same thing with his son. Bill suffered from depression in adulthood largely because of his denial of these qualities within himself — creativity, sensitivity, and the need to talk.

We need to practise radical acceptance of our children's nature. This means accepting them for who they are, not for who we want them to be or who we think they should be. Our children are not miniature versions of ourselves, and parenting is not a rerun of our own childhood. We will be able to accept our children for who they are when we are able to accept ourselves for who we are. To raise an emotionally healthy child, we have to be emotionally healthy ourselves, and this means accepting and living according to our own unique nature. It means looking at past hurts, reflecting on them, and letting them go.

Healing Our Inner Child

A mother or father must sometimes find the inner child in him or herself who did not receive adequate nurturing — and nurture that child. She must talk to that pouting child who sits with arms crossed and lip turned down. She must hug that child, hold that child. As parents, we must learn to love ourselves before we can fully love our children, and this might mean going back and feeding unmet needs. This is not easy to do because it doesn't happen in the real world. The child we once were only exists within us. We can only meet that child in the world of thought, emotion, and imagination. We have to think about our unmet needs from child-hood, we have to meditate on our losses, and we have to grieve for that little boy or girl who did not get enough. We have to acknowledge their existence or they will continue to pull at our shirt sleeves, distract us from the present, and drain our energy for the tasks at hand.

The Narcissistic Wound

Some parents find it hard to show unconditional love because they did not receive it themselves. Narcissus is a character in Greek mythology who fell in love with his own image reflected in a pool of water. He has become the archetype of the self-absorbed person, unable to show an interest in anyone but himself. Children are naturally narcissistic. Their own subjective experience is all they can process. They are not develop-mentally able to project themselves into the consciousness of another person to imagine what they might be feeling. For a very young child, "it's all about me!" and that's appropriate for the earliest stages of de-velopment. This narcissistic need must be met. Children can seem like bottomless pits of need, but these needs are valid and important.

When one's needs are not met in childhood, this narcissism can continue into adulthood. A person can spend the rest of their life look-ing for the affirmation they never received in childhood. We are able to love others when we love ourselves. We learn to love ourselves when we are loved by others — beginning with our primary caregivers. Sadly, some people receive very little love in childhood, and as a result they have a hard time showing it. A cycle of need is set up with the adult always looking for a love they never received as a child. The parent is not able to give unconditional love to his or her child, and that child grows up with the same inability. One of the greatest gifts we can give our children is the gift of nurturing affection, the gift of unconditional positive regard, the gift of love.

Narcissism is on the rise in our culture because so many adults did not have their narcissistic needs met in childhood. They were raised by busy parents who were physically or emotionally absent, who just did the best they could. We need to do better than this by being emotionally available to our children. Many parents find parenting difficult because they sometimes feel they have nothing left to give. They feel drained by their children. This is not a shortcoming or fault in the parent. It is the parent's story. The parent with narcissistic need did not choose to be this way and is often not even aware of it. All the parent knows is that he or she feels unprepared to give what is needed.

When I use a term like *narcissistic parent*, it may conjure up an image of a self-absorbed, insensitive, even cruel adult. This is not what I mean. This residual narcissism is a subtle wound left in almost everyone, to varying degrees. For a whole range of reasons — economic, social, personal — many of our parents were not able to give us everything we may have needed. The parent with a narcissistic wound who was unable to give unselfishly to the child produces a wounded adult who repeats the pattern. The adult turns to the child in the same way the adults in their childhood turned to them — seeking love.

Children of narcissistic parents are left with the daunting task of trying to break this cycle by re-parenting themselves. They must give to themselves what they did not get enough of in childhood — unconditional love. Children of narcissistic parents often grow up to be high achievers. They expect the same from their children. A person's value is measured by their performance and their accomplishments. These are things for which the child received praise and affirmation, so they become the currency of love and the content of self-esteem. It is performance-based esteem. They're as good as their last report card, their last goal in hockey, their last sticker, trophy, or ribbon. Children of narcissistic parents believe that if they just try harder, they will be loved.

They can spend their whole lives seeking the approval of others, which is a substitute for the unconditional love they did not receive in childhood. Adults who were raised by narcissistic parents have a child within who is not fully formed, who is arrested in his or her development, and who needs to be acknowledged and nurtured. If we fail to do this, we end up resenting our own children for the demands they make on us.

The Unconscious Parent

What we don't deal with we pass on. We want our children to be emotionally healthy but this depends on our own emotional health. We want our children to be happy, but their happiness depends upon our own happiness. Our children need us to deal with our own "stuff" before we can give them what they need. In my counselling of parents and children, I often find that the child's behaviour is a direct result of the parent's unresolved emotional issues. The parent brings the child to me to be "fixed," and there is nothing to fix. The child's behaviour is in reaction to the parent's conscious and unconscious core beliefs and behaviour. The child's negative behaviour becomes ingrained over many years, so that now, indeed, the child has a problem — but the whole dynamic began many years before.

Bonnie called me in desperation about her twelve-year-old son, Matthew. She said she was at the end of her rope. She didn't know what to do. "Our life is a mess. Every day is a battle. He won't do anything I ask. All I get is attitude." I spent several sessions with Matthew. We talked, played, and worked on homework. He was polite, intelligent, and focused. In one way, I was only seeing Matthew's public persona. He behaved for me because I was a stranger — an unfamiliar adult on whom he wanted to make a positive impression. But at the same time, we cannot dismiss his positive behaviour as false. It was very sincere behaviour, and it could even be argued that this was Matthew's "better self," which he was getting a chance to exercise outside of the family constellation. When Matthew and I were alone, I asked him what the problems at home were and he described the same kinds of behaviours his mother did. When I asked him what he thought was the cause of the problems at home, he truly could not answer. He was a very smart boy, but he truly seemed stumped by this question. The only thing he could think to say was "it's me." Matthew's answer was a little different from most kids who get to this point in the conversation. More often kids will say something like "it's my Mom" or "it's my parents," and then go on to enumerate their parents' shortcomings and irritating behaviours. Then I spoke with Matthew and his mother together. Matthew's behaviour changed completely — he became a sullen, disrespectful, angry child. "You see," said his mother. "This is what I deal with all the time."

Bonnie had grown up in a very authoritarian home where any attempt at self-regulation or autonomy was always shut down. Her father had total power and control over the whole family. As a little girl and a teenager, Bonnie railed against this oppressive atmosphere by means of external rebellion and inner anger that became depression. What she couldn't see was the way in which she had totally reproduced her own childhood dynamic with her son. She simply did not listen to him. She was constantly directing him, correcting him, and managing him. Whenever he expressed his point of view, she would point out what was wrong or inaccurate in his opinions. He could never win. Her verbal and intellectual abilities were beyond him, and he felt totally powerless. His only recourse was attitude. The great psychologist Viktor Frankl once said, "The one thing you can't take away from me is the way I choose to respond to what you do to me. The last of one's freedoms is to choose one's attitude in any given circumstance." This is the dynamic we see with many teenagers and it was certainly true for Matthew. The attitude he chose was defiance and rudeness. By the time I met them, Matthew and Bonnie had been living with this chemistry for many years. Each side was completely entrenched in their way of relating to the other. I felt very sad for both of them. He was not getting the love and nurturing he needed, and Bonnie was a nervous wreck. Bonnie seemed like a conscious parent in that she was constantly describing and analyzing her son's behaviour and trying to figure out strategies for dealing with it, but she was a completely unconscious parent in the sense that she seemed totally unaware of the way her own upbringing was influencing her parenting. When I raised the issue of her father's parenting style, she just shrugged it off; "Oh, I'm nothing like him." This is the great challenge of personal change and transformation. There can be a huge gap between what we think we know and what we actually know. There can also be a willful blindness about how we feel, think, and act. Bonnie was stuck in a loop. Her responses to her son became automatic. Viktor Frankl had something to say about this too: "Between stimulus and response, there is a space. In that space is our power to choose our response. In our response lies our growth and our freedom."

For many conscious parents, parenting happens on two levels. There is the external day-to-day level of the hundreds of tiny interactions with our children, and then there is the inner level where we consciously or unconsciously recall parallel situations in our own childhoods. As we raise our own children, it can be like watching a rerun of our own lives. We naturally compare then and now, and sometimes the past can cloud our perceptions of the present. We need to be careful as parents that we do not unconsciously reproduce any negative parenting we received or let our resentments or anger about particular childhood experiences taint our enjoyment of the present. We can re-parent ourselves by the way we parent our children. When we come to them with unconditional love we are in essence saying to our own inner child that this is the kind of treatment we deserve — and did deserve. We didn't get it then, but we give it to ourselves now. When we come to our child with nurturing affection, we nurture our inner child. When we listen attentively and empathetically to our children, we are affirming ourselves. When we champion our child we are, at the same time, championing our own inner child who may never have received such support. When we honour our child's unique nature, we are saying to ourselves that it was okay to be the way we were, and it's okay to be the way we are. We may not have been fully appreciated at the time, so we did not appreciate ourselves. Once we can appreciate who we are, we can appreciate who our children are — each one unique.

Be Yourself

Most of us grew up in a world, in a school system in particular, that valued sameness, where conformity and fitting in were top priorities.

This made it hard to accept, develop, or champion that which was unique, different, or unusual about us. These were things that needed pruning. Many of us were heavily pruned in the name of adjustment and socialization. The "well-adjusted" child can grow up to be a very neurotic child when their true nature is not honoured. When we see creative adults who are leading interesting lives, we are often looking at people who refused to adjust, or who grew up in an environment where the imperative to adjust was not present. If neither of these two reasons explains why the adult is so free, it is because the adult has done the long and difficult work of overcoming or undoing all those years of adjustment. The adult has had to unlearn all those lessons about fitting in, conforming, and pleasing others at the expense of the true self. We do our child a great service when we spare them this arduous task in adulthood. Instead of having to find out who they really are at midlife, wouldn't it be nice for them to grow up always in touch with who they really are, and not only in touch with it but actually enjoying it and living it? This is the great gift we can give our children.

Take Care of Our Sustaining Relationships

Accepting our true nature and taking care of our emotional health is a project fed by sustaining relationships. In our fast-paced world, many women and men feel lonely and isolated. They may be separated from extended family; they may have few friends; they may feel emotionally unsatisfied in their marriage or relationship. Men may take refuge in work or escape into cyber-space. For women, the convenient substitute for adult love is often found nearby in the love of children. When either parent depends on their children for sustaining relationships, emotional boundaries become blurred. The role of surrogate partner or surrogate friend is too big a role for a child to play. In order to raise emotionally healthy children, we need to take care of our own emotional health, and this means working on our relationships with other adults including our romantic relationships. We must never take our sustaining relationships for granted. When a parent becomes socially and emotionally isolated, it is not good for children.

Our Unresolved Need for Power and Control

Another area where we can end up working out unresolved issues is in our need for power and control. Many of the problems between children and adults, both in the home and at school, boil down to these two things. Power and control become ends in themselves, not means to an end. As we grow into adulthood we learn that power and control are rare and valuable commodities that must be held on to at any cost. We learn this from a very early age by having power and control repeatedly taken from us by adults who have also learned this grim lesson. Parenting strategies seem to begin with the question, "How can I keep my power and control?" and not, "What's best for the child?" If we did ask this question, we would give the child more opportunities to practise power and control. Ideally, that is what we want to teach children — how to assume power and control in a responsible manner, where it goes by names like autonomy, self-regulation, self-directedness, independence. The only way they will learn these qualities is by having opportunities to practise them. If their power and control are constantly being thwarted, this only breeds resentment and an even greater desire for these two things. As children feel more controlled, monitored, and managed, they become more neurotic in their ways of seeking power and control.

The issue of power and control in child-rearing has huge social implications. To what extent are the need to make money (corporate greed), the need to control nature (environmental damage), and the need to control others (sexual assault) the result of child-rearing practices that deny children healthy and productive expressions of power and control? These destructive behaviours by adults may be manifestations of something they were denied in childhood. In the extreme, when one reads the biography of almost any political dictator, one finds an authoritarian parent who robbed the child of any sense of power and control. The template for that person's life is set — achieve power and control over others at any cost. On a less extreme level, the schoolyard bully is looking for the same thing. We have all worked under bosses whose main priority seemed to be maintaining power and control over others. This does not make for a very pleasant workplace. Psychologists have shown us that the sexual and physical assault of women and children is, at root, motivated by a need for power and control. Therefore we can see that power and control are not trivial issues in child-rearing. They go to the core of many of our social problems. The way we raise our children has huge implications for the kind of society we end up living in. Maria Montessori believed that in the way we raise children lies the way to world peace. This may seem like a grand claim, but I absolutely agree.

Seeing Our Children for Who They Really Are

One of the most profound needs that all children have is the need to be seen. It has been shown that when a baby comes out of the womb, one of the first things it does is look for its mother's eyes. When the baby sees its mother's eyes, the baby relaxes. The baby knows on some very deep level that it's okay, that the world is not a hostile place. "I am safe," it feels. "I am loved." Even more important, researchers tell us that the child continues to do this during all of its developmental phases — looking first to mother and then to all caregivers and significant others' eyes for messages about the world and messages about one's value as a person. Psychologists call it mirroring. We know we exist because we see ourselves first in the eyes of others. We know we have value because we see an expression of love in those eyes. The great American psychologist Carl Rogers defined love as *unconditional positive regard*. When we receive this, the foundation of our self-esteem is laid. When we sense that others are not really seeing us, we become insecure. Sometimes the adults in our lives do not see us for who we really are. They see us for who they expect us to be, who they hope we will be, who the neighbours expect, who the in-laws expect — the list of expectations could go on at length. While satisfying the expectations of others can bring praise and affirmation, it is ultimately a hollow experience, because one's deeper nature ends up being ignored and neglected. As time goes on, these expectations can eat away at the child's self-perception. "I am lacking in some way," he thinks. "There are things I was supposed to become that I have not." Sometimes we're not even sure what those things were supposed to be. We are just left with a pervasive sense of never being good enough. Some of us become "people pleasers," praise junkies who are always seeking the approval or unconditional positive regard of others. The sad and frustrating part is that the positive regard that we people pleasers receive is not unconditional. It is conditional upon our behaviour. We hear not "I love you" but "I will love you if you behave in ways I like. I will love you if your values and opinions are the same as mine. I will love you if you live out the script I have planned for you." The first and most powerful thing we can do for a boy is to see him for who he really is and to love him for who he is.

Following the Crowd

We need to think about the kind of parenting we had, and we need to make conscious choices about the kind of parenting we want to practise. The world has changed a lot since our own parents raised us. We cannot go to them and ask them how they dealt with video games or cell phones. We cannot remember how they talked to us about school shootings or internet pornography. In so many ways, today's parents are making it up as they go along. We need to educate ourselves about the issues, talk about them with each other, and reflect on them individually. We need to make conscious choices about how to raise our children, or else other people, other forces, will make those choices for us.

One of the default modes of human beings is to fall back on the wisdom of the herd, to simply buy into collective values because we don't have the time or energy to think things through for ourselves. This leaves us at the mercy of conformity where the best parent is the one who does what everyone else is doing. The bad parent is the one who does things a little differently. This is a dangerous situation not only for parents but for children who end up adopting this approach to life. "If you're ever unsure of what to do," they learn, "just do what everyone else is doing." Consumer capitalism is another contributing factor in our confusion about parenting and life in general. We are constantly being told what we should want and what we should do. The opinions of the herd are largely formed by advertising.

The American Academy of Pediatrics has repeatedly said that television and other entertainment media should be avoided for infants and children under age two, and yet countless programs and even apps have been created for children in this age group. The following appeared on Parents.com, whose parent company, the Meredith Corporation, boasts on its corporate website that it reaches over 100 million American women through its print and digital magazines:

> In recent years, parents everywhere have learned that no matter how many toys, books, and instruments that they purchase for their babies and toddlers, there's one device that never grows old: the cell phone.
>
> To make sense of all the apps out there aimed at kids, we turned to tech expert Katie Linendoll (talknerdytome. net) who is a regular contributor on CNN and *The Early Show*, to share some of her favorites.
>
> "I call the iPad the ultimate babysitter," says Linendoll. "Because it's very easy to use, there's no manual, and when the price point is typically free or 99 cents, you can't go wrong in downloading a bunch and seeing what you like."

The tone of these kinds of articles is so confident and robust, one would never think of questioning what is actually being said — that cell phone apps are the best way to keep a baby quiet and occupied! To be a conscious parent, to maintain one's individual perspective, is harder today than it has ever been.

Dare to Be Different

What kids need to see are adults who live according to values that are not those of the herd. They need to see adults who live free and independent lives even when that means sticking out in some way. The unspoken thesis of every advertisement is "fit in — and we will show you how." *Fashion* and *style* were words once used to describe changes over decades or centuries. They are now used to describe changes over weeks or months. And what is in or out is not just applied to clothing or hairstyles but to almost every consumer product. It is called built-in obsolescence. The minute we buy the next big thing, there is another one to take its place. Our social status is determined by the things we own. We become confused and depressed when we can't keep up. What is far more tragic is that we become alienated from our own tastes, our own desires, and our own perceptions of reality. We like what we are told to like and avoid everything else. We think we are free to choose what we want, and yet so many of our wants have been dictated to us by advertising. As Steve Jobs said, "People don't know what they want until you show it to them." We become like trained animals lining up waiting for the store to open so we can be the first one to own a thing — knowing full well that it will be outdated by the afternoon.

We worry about our kids giving in to peer pressure, and yet as adults we do it every day. If we want our kids to make conscious, responsible choices, if we want them to be able to stand on their own two feet and trust their own perceptions, then we must model this kind of behaviour ourselves, not just encouraging them to "be yourself" but by doing this ourselves and making sure it's visible to our children. We need to articulate to them the reasons for the choices we make to show them that everything we do is a choice. Even when we conform to a social norm, that can be a choice. It does not have to be an automatic reflex, an unconscious conditioned response. We can accept or reject a piece of clothing even though it has the coolest designer logo. In the same way, we can accept or reject the marijuana joint being passed even though it's the coolest kid at school passing it.

2

The Need to Be Listened To

Listening is an act of humility. To listen is to put our own outputs on hold in order to receive someone else's. For so many people listening means "waiting for the other person to finish so that I can say what I have lined up to say." To truly receive what someone else is saying in an open and non-judgmental way — just to receive it — is a rare act. We tend to bring a very utilitarian approach to listening. We think there has to be some outcome, some product. We come to believe that listening to someone else is a stimulus for what we're going to say next — either about ourselves, or in response to what the other person has just said. Sometimes listening does not demand a response. It only demands attention to the other person. The other person may not necessarily want advice or want to hear our parallel experience. They may just want someone to receive what they are saying. This simple act can be very validating. "I hear you," it says. "Your words have value. You have value." People, including kids, have a great capacity to solve their own problems once they see them laid out on the table. This is what we do when we listen well. We give someone the opportunity to lay their cards on the table and look at them for themselves.

Sometimes a parent's first response to what a child says is to point out its inaccuracy or to turn it into a lesson.

Grade four child: "Michael got in trouble again at school today. He took something off the teacher's desk."

Parent: "Well, Michael is going to have to learn not to touch other people's things."

We take the experience of the child and we package it. We make sense of it for them. We pre-empt any processing on the child's part. An alternative to the blunt summing-up of what the child has said is to say nothing and see where the child will go with it. I usually find that the child is capable of taking the thought process quite far. Parenting expert Barbara Coloroso says we should teach our children how to think not what to think. So much of what we say to children is really rooted in our own need, our own processes. The response from the parent above is an expression of what he or she thought about the reported behaviour. We think out loud in front of the child and short-circuit their cognitive processing. It can be a great gift to a child to let them continue. The fact that the child raised the scenario at all indicates it has meaning for the child, that there is something in the event that they would like to work through. If the child does not spontaneously pursue the topic, we can draw out the implications of the event through subtle questioning.

- "What did he take?"
- "What did the teacher say?"
- "What did Michael do afterward?"
- "Has anything like that ever happened to you?"
- "Why do you think Michael did it?"
- "Why do you think the teacher got mad?"
- "Do you think Michael was trying to be bad?"

The scenario described is about boundaries and impulsive behaviour. These are core issues for children. "Where are the limits? What is right and wrong? What will the consequences be if I transgress the boundaries? When do I need to control my impulses? How do I control my impulses? What will happen if I don't control them? What are the rewards if I do?" The best way for a child to answer these questions is through their own thought processes which the adult can facilitate — not dictate.

Fast Talk, Slow Talk

One of the most important things I learned in talking with children was the need to slow myself down. As a teacher in the classroom I knew only too well how talking could be used as a tool for external control. For parents too, talking is one of our main modes of control. Sometimes it seems we are constantly giving instructions and directions, and making comments on things. This is a fundamental part of being a parent, but it is not the only thing we need to do. We need to stop, look, and listen, and this entails slowing down the flow of language. This is a particular issue for mothers (and female teachers) who, brain research tells us, produce language much more quickly and easily than males do (generally speaking). When women talk to boys or men, they need to slow the flow, not just in the production of words, but in the time given for the other person to process and say something in response. Watch a conversation between a parent and child and try to monitor the language processing speed of each participant. You will notice that the adult has a much faster and more sophisticated flow. The child may struggle to keep up. Children have a very different rhythm from adults, not to mention a different vocabulary. The context has a lot to do with it. There are conversations that happen as we are getting boots, coats, and hats on to go out the door. There may be no time to slow down the rate of words in this situation. Then there are those conversations that happen while snuggling in bed or on the couch or at the dinner table where the parent is relaxed enough to slow down. These are the times when the best conversations can happen.

In talking with boys, we have to learn to wait. We have to be comfortable with silence. In my one-on-one work with boys, I think the thing most observers would notice are the periods of silence, the times in between when nothing is said because both of us are thinking — thinking about what was just said or what we want to say next. It always amazes me what comes out when I am quiet and wait. Jeremy was fourteen years old and having a hard time in grade nine. He was suffering from a lot of anxiety, and his marks were going down. He told me that he found school "too much" sometimes. When we talked more about this, he described how hard it was to be at his locker and have all the kids around him talking. Some would be talking to him and some not and he couldn't even always tell the difference. He found it hard to "come up with something to say" quickly. He said that one of the reasons he liked coming to his mentoring sessions was that it was quiet and the talking was slow. He had a chance to think about what he wanted to say. I have had many adolescent boys report the same thing.

During adolescence, testosterone levels increase quickly and significantly. It has been shown that testosterone inhibits language production in the brain. If parents of teenagers and high school teachers were more aware of this phenomenon, there would be a lot less conflict with boys. Boys need more time to formulate their thoughts, and they do not formulate them as well when they are stressed. When parents and teens fight, the teenage boy can feel a huge disadvantage and a sense of powerlessness in his inability to come up with a good comeback. His parents can throw all kinds of logical arguments at him, and he just doesn't have the capacity to process these ideas quickly, much less come back with strong counter-arguments. This is why he will simply shut down, leave the room, or become aggressive. He feels it is a no-win situation, and he's right. When talking to a stressed male, we need to slow things down, back off, and wait. Sometimes we need to wait until later in the day or the next day when the stress has passed.

Non-Verbal Communication

Many younger children do not have the verbal sophistication to articulate the thoughts and feelings going on inside them. They are either too young or they simply do not have the vocabulary to differentiate between the various feelings they are having. Their emotional lives are like a kaleidoscope of colours. There is a pattern, but it is complex and constantly changing. For a child to capture this cascading variety in words is just too difficult. When communicating with children, we have to relearn the power of non-verbal communication. We all had it as children ourselves, but most of us lost much of it when we developed sophisticated language. Profound communication can occur when two people are simply *doing* something together. A child and I will often draw together or play with Lego. There is very little talk, but I know it is both bonding and therapeutic. Sometimes there is talking, and the subject can be important or trivial. What the child is drawing or making always has meaning *for the child*. I may not know what that meaning is, but that ultimately doesn't matter. The child is getting something out. They are taking something inside themselves and making it real outside themselves. This can happen through words, but it can also happen in other ways — using pictures, clay, actions, and play. When two people are together, there is some kind of exchange going on even if they are not talking. At the deepest level, one could use spiritual language and say that heart speaks to heart or soul speaks to soul — I certainly believe this to be true. When we do something quietly with a child, and especially when we allow the child to take the lead, we are giving them a great gift. We are attending to them. We are affirming their will. We are strengthening the esteem they have for themselves.

Parents need to trust in this kind of communication. The female brain generally prefers words. The male brain is typically more comfortable with actions as a mode of communication and therefore more comfortable with silence. Mothers need to trust that deep communication can occur when there is no talking. Women sometimes wish that their husbands (or their teenage sons) would be more verbal. "Use your words," they say. Men and boys often communicate more easily through their actions. Doing something for someone can be a male's way of saying "I love you." Of course words have their value, but we need to reclaim the value of actions, of non-verbal communication, which may say even more than words could.

The child who is acting out is communicating something to us non-verbally. Whether he's running around in circles, hitting his sister, or retreating to his room, all of these behaviours are an expression of something going on inside. Some children flap their hands when they are excited, happy, or nervous. They are getting their feelings out or *discharging affect*. Or think of the angry child who lies on his back and waves his legs in the air. These are just two examples of powerful and effective non-verbal communication. The adult's job is to listen to or read these behaviours. Is the child angry, bored, or anxious? Is the child content, excited, or happy? All behaviour is logical, which means it can be explained if we know how to read it and all behaviour is an expression of our inner state. When we are trying to interpret the reasons behind a particular behaviour, we must be cautious about always defaulting to a negative interpretation. Sometimes running around in circles means "I'm happy." Sometimes hitting a sister means "I love being with her and I want more of her attention." Retreating into one's room may mean "I'm feeling peaceful and content." It is the job of the wise adult to interpret the behaviour of the child objectively. We often project our own feelings onto the child. Is the child angry, bored, or anxious or are *you* angry, bored, or anxious? One of the biggest challenges for parents is seeing our children objectively, not through the lens of our own feelings, especially our stress and anxiety.

Parental Stress and Anxiety

We need to be in touch with our own feelings as well as those of our children. When we are overwhelmed with an emotion, we cannot see the emotions of others clearly. Everything becomes coloured by the emotion we are feeling. Stress and anxiety are two of the strongest feelings that can disrupt a parent's ability to see their child clearly. Parents need to deal with their own stress and anxiety before they can be totally present with their children. I advise time-outs for parents just as much as for kids. Sometimes we simply need to remove ourselves from the situation. Our less-than-best self is probably going to come out if we speak, so don't let it. If we are suffering from chronic stress or anxiety, then we need to deal with it — for our children's sake. We will end up communicating our stress and anxiety both in verbal and non-verbal ways. The three most immediate and effective ways of dealing with stress in our lives are sleep, exercise, and talk. When we're tired we are automatically stressed. Exercise releases dopamine and endorphins, the feel-good hormones. Talking with another person untangles the wires in the head. When we ruminate, we think ourselves into a knot. Through talking, we can untangle that knot and make our energy flow again. Here are two simple questions to ask ourselves about chronic stress: What is the cause of my stress, and what can I do to change it? Sometimes just naming our stressors is the biggest step. When the necessary changes are big, we can start with little-picture, short-term solutions and move on later to big-picture, long-term solutions — but we can always start somewhere to change our lives for the better.

For seven years I commuted over a thousand kilometers a week. I would leave around six o'clock in the morning and get home around six at night. I loved reading to the kids at night after dinner, but it was really hard to stay awake! I was stressed and frustrated. But living far from work was an economic necessity — we simply could not afford the house prices nearer to Toronto. Finally, the stress and wear and tear on my body became too much. I injured a nerve in my neck, and that was the final straw — we decided to sell the house and just rent a place closer to Toronto. It was the best thing that could have happened. I reclaimed over two hours a day in my life and our whole lifestyle changed. I see many parents suffering from low-level chronic stress created by lifestyle choices combined with economic pressures. Most of us feel as though we have no choice. This is not as true as we think. We become trapped in conventional attitudes and paths. In my own case, we ended up renting a farmhouse within walking distance of the school where I worked. The house was pretty run down and required a lot of work, but I think our whole family would agree that the six years we spent living there were among the happiest and most interesting in our family's life.

As our children express themselves non-verbally, so do we — without even knowing it. Our body language is much more subtle than theirs. Instead of lying on the floor screaming, we express ourselves in subtle gestures, facial expressions, and tones of voice. Because children are so intuitive and pre-verbal, they pick up our non-verbal messages very quickly. They pick up our stress, our frustration, our anger — even when our words are saying nothing about these things, even when we try to cover up our true emotional state with rosy words and fake smiles. Again, we are faced with the deep challenge of parenting: to become our best selves, to deal with our stress, to become healthy and whole. If we think we can fake it with our kids or just get by, we are not being honest with ourselves or with them. Parenting is a huge challenge, but it is also an incredible opportunity for personal growth.

3

The Sensory Child

We all begin life as totally sensual beings. The external world comes pouring in through many avenues — sight, taste, touch, smell, sound, the feel of our own bodies from within, our emotions, our perceptions. As adults, we would be overwhelmed if we could get back inside the mind and body of a baby or a young toddler and perceive the world with that level of intensity again. The story of growing up is the story of shutting down and closing off many of those doors of perception. We are conditioned to feel less (stop crying) and to sense less (don't touch) as we grow up. We become more limited, and more neurotic. So many of the decisions we make in child-rearing are decisions in favour of adjusting to the demands of the group — however unhealthy or unrealistic these demands might be. Children (and the rest of us) pay a high price when we become *too* civilized or *too* socialized. The question is how can we keep more of our children's good, healthy, natural inclinations alive? We can promote emotional, mental, and physical health by better understanding what is natural in children — honouring it and managing it rather than trying to extinguish it. We use training, punishment, shame, and medication to turn kids into something they are not. Many parenting books have a hidden subtext: How to Control Your Child. How to Fix Your Child. How to Make Your Child Normal. We talk about the well-adjusted child as though it were high praise, but we must ask ourselves what they have adjusted to and what may have been lost in the process of adjusting. Two things that often get lost are their emotional selves and their sensual selves — and this is particularly true for boys.

For the past ten years, I have worked as a tutor, mentor, and coach to many kids diagnosed with Attention Deficit Disorder (ADD) and Attention Deficit Hyperactivity Disorder (ADHD). Some of my clients use medication; others do not. My sessions with these kids last an hour, and many of these kids simply cannot focus on anything for longer than five or ten minutes. The symptoms manifest in their bodies — squirminess, walking around, impulsive behaviours of all kinds. Parents ask me for strategies and advice. I became interested in non-medical interventions for ADD/ADHD and a couple of mothers introduced me to sensory-processing theory. Originally developed by Jean Ayres and popularized by Carol Kranowitz in her book *The Out-of-Sync Child*, this theory has become an important part of physiotherapy with children but has important implications for the generation of screen-loving kids who often exhibit the symptoms of ADD/ADHD even though they don't have it.

As we grow, we must learn to integrate all of our sensory inputs. The brain becomes like an orchestra conductor or a traffic cop — directing and integrating all of this information. By the time we reach adulthood we have, for the most part, integrated all of our sensory inputs. We are good sensory processors. How did we get this way? We did it by exercising all of our senses on a regular basis: sight, hearing, smell, taste, touch. In addition, Kranowitz emphasizes three other senses we don't hear much about: the proprioceptive sense (our sense of our muscles and joints), the vestibular sense (our sense of balance), and the interoceptive sense (our awareness of our internal organs). We became good sensory processors because we grew up with a rich *sensory diet*. Many kids today are growing up with a poor sensory diet. As boys spend more and more time on screens, the only sense that really gets a work out is the sense of sight. As a result of a poor sensory diet, we see problem behaviours in boys ranging from inattentiveness, hyperactivity, and distractibility to poor social functioning. Children who have difficulty processing their sensory experience can become overwhelmed, distracted, unable to focus, or stressed — all of which can lead to acting out in various ways. The child is overstimulated because they have not learned how to manage all the information coming in — the process referred to as sensory integration.

Sensory processing is developed by exercising as many of the senses as possible. Children will naturally gravitate toward those sensory experiences that their body needs to exercise. Why would I walk down the hall when I could spin down the hall (vestibular sense)? When standing in line it's more fun if we push and shove each other (the proprioceptive sense). According to Dr. Ayers, "Sensations that make a child happy tend to be integrating." Exercises that integrate the senses include a whole range of activities that do not require any equipment, training, or adult supervision — for the simple reason that they are natural. Here is a list:

- Playing with water
- Playing with sand
- Touching different textures
- Getting a back rub, a bear hug, or a hand or foot massage
- Wrestling
- Rough-housing
- Play fighting
- Spinning
- Rolling
- Hopping
- Somersaulting
- Rocking
- Jumping
- Swinging
- Balancing on a board or ball
- Running
- Stretching
- Lifting
- Pushing
- Pulling
- Hanging by the arms
- Extending and flexing the joints

For kids with attention-control issues, sensory-processing theory presents a way of responding to the pent up energy of the child who is trying to focus on a task while his body wants to run and squirm and wiggle. There are many exercises that enhance sensory processing. Sitting on a swivel chair or ball-chair allows the child to move his feet while sitting. Having something in the hand to squeeze or the gentle squeezing of the hands or feet themselves all help a child to focus better. As Kranowtiz shows, the hands and feet contain large numbers of sensory receptors connected to both the sensory cortex and the motor cortex of the brain. The hands and feet are natural pathways to the brain and the attention control center. Stimulating them serves to override or drown out other sensory inputs. When the child focuses on the tactile pressure or movement of the hands or feet, other inputs recede into the background. With these techniques, kids are able to maintain a focused conversation, to read, or to listen while being read to, and are generally calmer, more verbal, and more focused.

We see sensory-processing theory at work in other ways as well. Some children work better when listening to music . The sense of hearing is overstimulated and all other inputs recede into the background. The child calms and is better able to focus. In the same way, video games overstimulate the visual sense causing other sensory inputs to recede. A child playing video games is able to hyperfocus because of this overstimulation of one sense. We see the same phenomenon in thumb-sucking or when children caress certain parts of their bodies. We call these behaviours self-comforting. They are part of the process of sensory integration for a growing child.

Some children experience hyper(high)-sensitivity in one area or hypo(low)-sensitivity in another area.

- A child who is hyper-sensitive to touch may be bothered by clothing tags or want to wear the same clothes all the time.
- A child who is hyper-sensitive to taste may be a picky eater or hate brushing their teeth.
- A child who is hyper-sensitive to sound may cover his or her ears or be very sensitive to yelling (or what they perceive to be yelling).

- The hyper-sensitive child tends to prefer low-risk activities.
- A child who is hypo-sensitive needs more sensual stimulation to get the same feeling another child would get with less. He may be a bumper, a banger, and a crasher (hyperactivity). He may like spicy foods, loud music, and high-risk activities.

Seven-year-old Connor is a toucher. He does not really believe he has seen something until he touches it. His hands are just as important to his understanding of the world as his eyes. He finds great pleasure in touching and being touched. Ever since he entered school, there has been a daily effort to get him to stop touching other people, objects in the classroom, and his own body. What does this daily effort teach a child, and what will the long-term effects be? He learns that there is something wrong with him, and that touch is a bad thing. Whenever the topic is raised, his face takes on a guilty expression. He has been shamed many times about his natural desires. While children do need to learn about socially acceptable behaviour, they should not be shamed out of their intrinsic way of relating to the world. I practise sensory processing exercises with Connor whenever he comes to see me. I squeeze his hands, flap his arms, give him bear hugs, or squeeze his feet. He finds great pleasure in this, but more importantly, he feels affirmed and accepted. The child must be led gently to a compromise between what he or she wants and what the world expects. For some children, this process takes longer than it does for others.

Some kids have a stronger tactile need than others, or perhaps it would be more accurate to say they hold on to this need longer than others. We have a low tolerance for the child who does not develop in sync with his peer group. We immediately see it as a problem to be solved. This is a by-product of our education system, which segregates children by age. All five year olds are put together in a room and are expected to behave more or less the same way. The sad truth is that eventually they will, but this does not mean it is natural. Those who are ahead of their peer group may slow down or become frustrated; those who are behind their peer group may feel compelled to let go of "childish" behaviours they may not be ready to let go of. They may feel sad at having to do so and inadequate for finding it hard. They might also feel inadequate about not being able to do some of the cognitive tasks the other kids can do. It is interesting to note that we often equate "immature" behaviour with lower intelligence. Connor's behaviour would be judged the most immature in the class, yet his psycho-educational assessment shows that he is the most intelligent. Connor's cognitive development is progressing at a rapid rate, but he simply refuses to let some of the pleasurable behaviours of childhood go. I admire his tenacity and his integrity. He refuses to give up what he values. He refuses to give in to arbitrary norms of behaviour. This is a very positive trait that should be affirmed and accommodated.

Sensory-processing theory can also help us understand the picky eater. Many kids are picky eaters simply because their taste buds are extra sensitive. Just the colour or texture of a food can be overwhelming, not to mention the taste. One of the most powerful sensory and motor connections in the brain is with the mouth. I was an extremely picky eater, and it drove my mother crazy. She was a child of the depression when kids had to eat everything on their plates. Throwing food out was not an option — so, instead, I would throw it across the room! Thankfully this was a rare occurrence, but the more common scenario was that I was left sitting at the table for hours after everyone had left. It became a battle of wills. It was no longer about food. It was about winning the battle. For me at that age the battle was worth fighting. The taste and feel of certain foods was just intolerable.

Back then, such behaviour was labelled *stubborn*. Today we have new labels. Avoidant/Restrictive Food Intake Disorder (ARFID) was introduced as a new diagnostic category in the revised Diagnostic and Statistical Manual of Mental Disorders — Fifth Edition (DSM-V) of the American Psychiatric Association. Isaac is a ten-year-old boy whose diet consists almost exclusively of chicken fingers, Goldfish crackers, pancakes, and muffins. He will accept these foods because they do not overstimulate his highly sensitive palette. His mother was one of the first to mention sensory processing to me. Unlike my childhood experience, there is no nagging, arguing, or throwing of food in Isaac's house. The parents understand their child's sensitivity. They work on slowly expanding his repertoire and in the meantime make sure to supplement his limited diet with vitamins and minerals.

Jack is fifteen years old and will only wear one kind of T-shirt and one kind of pants. The T-shirt must fit tightly around the neck and have no printed decals. His pants must be loose fitting but must have elastic at the ankles. His mother makes no complaints. She buys him what he wants. It is this kind of tolerance and understanding that kids with high sensitivity require. I find that most kids will grow out of these needs, particularly around puberty when the body changes so much and peer pressure becomes a motivator. Having said that, we must still be sensitive and respectful of the adolescent, and indeed the adult, who continues to have sensory processing issues like these.

One of the common denominators I notice in children with sensory processing issues is their strong will. They are very clear about their own needs and limitations because their bodies send them such strong messages. They often suffer a lot of criticism and intolerance of their unique natures, and yet they stand firm. I see this as an admirable quality that will serve them well in life. They are not easily manipulated or swayed.

4

Discipline: Freedom, Structure, and Control

Parents complain about their strong-willed children. They use the word *stubborn*. It is a negative word for a positive quality. One of the greatest qualities a person can possess is a strong will. People with a strong will are competent, resilient, persevering, and successful. They lead dynamic lives. They know what they want and they go for it. The fact that they do not deal well with frustration can be seen as a good thing. They do not let it deter or defeat them. They fight through it until they get what they want. Strong-willed people are very goal-oriented. So if being strong-willed is such a good thing, why do parents complain about it in their children? The answer is very simple. The parent may be just as strong-willed (sometimes more), making the child a frustrating obstacle that stands in their way.

"But you can't always let them have their own way."

"I don't want to spoil him."

"I can't let him think he can have whatever he wants."

Here we stand at one of the most important boundary lines in parenting with freedom on one side of the line and external control on the other. As parents, we will always have to be moving back and forth across this line. Parents should try to move to the freedom side of the line whenever possible; however, there are times when we have to stand on the side of external control. At such times, the child is either too young or not able for other reasons (such as overwhelmed emotions) to make reasonable choices. In these cases the parent must step in and play the controlling role. Sometimes there are also external constraints that do, in fact, limit our freedom. They can be physical, social, or abstract. "I need to get to work. You need to get dressed. There are other kids waiting for a turn. You need to come off the swing. You are spending too many hours on Xbox."

When we lament the struggles involved in raising a strong-willed child, we should consider the alternative: a passive, overly compliant child. This kind of child may be easy to control, but is this the kind of child we want to raise? As strong-willed parents we can get stuck in control mode and mistake that for good parenting. Over-controlled children never learn to take responsibility for their own actions. They just learn obedience and adult-pleasing. They have no agenda of their own. Their job is to do what they're told. They might remain in that mode forever, never taking any initiative for themselves, never knowing or being able to articulate what their own hopes and dreams are ... their hopes and dreams are given to them by others.

Some children break this spell in adolescence by rebelling against external control. They become fed up with it and push back. We can see this as a disaster because it challenges our power and control, or we can see it as a healthy attempt to achieve autonomy. With adolescents in particular, we find ourselves back at the line with freedom on one side and external control on the other. We have another chance to teach responsibility through freedom. Too often, parents opt for external control. The teen is not listened to, is not taken seriously, and there is no attempt at negotiation and compromise. We do not serve our kids well when we shut them down. We need to teach them how to use their freedom responsibly, and the only way they can do that is by allowing them to practise it within safe boundaries.

Boundaries: Freedom Within Structure

Boys need both freedom *and* structure. These words sound like opposites, so another way of putting it is freedom *within* structure. The structures and routines we create are like the cup that holds the water. It is hard to drink out of the tap or out of our hands. Containers are all those structures we create to make life more manageable, to help us accomplish our goals. Problems arise when we focus more on the container than we do on the water. Sometimes we focus so much on structures and routine that freedom, creativity, and spontaneity are lost. Too much time spent on structure indicates an inordinate desire to maintain power and control. We must always be on guard against this tendency in ourselves. Children bring it out in us. They are so free and spontaneous that we feel we have to provide the antidote. This is when we become a stifling influence. We always have to maintain a balance between freedom and structure. We have to know where the boundaries are, name them, and then relax inside of them. Anything involving water helps to illustrate this — like painting or baking with a child. We set up the situation: for painting we put newspapers down on the table, we have the jar of water and the paints ready, the child puts an old adult shirt over his clothes. Now that the structure has been created, let the fun begin. Relax into the situation. When the child starts to paint his own hands, our hands, or our faces, then we have to decide how much we are willing or able to tolerate. We can invoke Barbara Coloroso's three questions: Is it harmful to the child? Is it harmful to others? Does it violate a moral code? If the answer to all three questions is no, then go ahead and enjoy. Sometimes a situation isn't necessarily harmful but it is inconvenient. "I don't have the time to wash him or myself after the painting session, so let's just keep it on the paper today."

The boundaries and consequences we have in our homes are all examples of structure or containers. Rules represent the limits. Consequences give those limits meaning. Within those limits lots of freedom is possible. Curfews are a good example. When a child is old enough to be out with friends alone, we can't control his behaviour. What we can still control is the limit on this time. Curfews are important limits to enforce from an early age. The other boundary is verbal abuse. When we do not tolerate our children calling us or each other names or making fun of others or bullying others with words, we are teaching the important skill of boundary setting. When we tell our children we will not tolerate being spoken to a certain way or say we will not allow him to speak to his sister or brother that way, we are teaching the importance of putting limits on what we will accept. The child can then copy this in his own life. If he is verbally abused at school, for example, he can apply the same boundary definition that he learned from us. He will be able to decide what he is willing to accept and what he is not willing to accept.

Self-Regulation

Our ultimate goal is not to raise an obedient child who sits passively in the various pens in which we place him. This is no recipe for effective adult functioning. Sadly, it is a common paradigm in parenting, in our school system, and in the workplace — the ideal child or adult is the one who takes direction well, who doesn't talk back, and who has no strong will of their own. We want children who are easy to manage, and by default we raise adults who are easy to manage. The situation becomes more problematic when the word *manage* is replaced with *manipulate*. Our ultimate goal is to raise a self-regulating child who will become a self-regulating adult, someone who knows what to do when we are not there to tell him what to do. This is why the freedom part of "freedom within structure" is so important. Kids need to feel their autonomy and exercise it. They need to learn that ultimately they are the masters of their own fate — nobody else. They must learn that they are responsible for the choices they make, but they can only learn this if they are free to make their own choices in the first place. When children don't follow our orders, we say they are making "bad choices," but is this true? They are making a choice to reject the dictates of another person. This could be seen as a positive and healthy thing. Sometimes when we say a child needs better *self-regulation,* we mean the child needs to be better at "doing what I want him to do." The grade-one boy who is rolling around on the floor during story time is self-regulating. He would like to be running around the room, but he is regulating his behaviour by choosing just to roll around on the floor instead. If this is too disruptive for the adult in the situation, then it is up to the person dictating the rules to justify their validity. If the adult cannot do this, then maybe the rule has no point. If the child is too young or too inexperienced to see the value of the rule, then the adult is justified in overriding the will of the child.

Some parents (and teachers) micromanage every aspect of their children's life. The children move and speak hesitantly when the parent is around because they know everything they say and do is being monitored and could be commented upon at any time. These children are so highly regulated that they do not get the opportunity to learn self-regulation. When the parent is not around, their behaviour can take one of two forms: total passivity — not knowing what to do when not being constantly told ; or rebellious, disruptive, anti-social behaviour — suddenly releasing all the pent up willpower that has never been able to find expression.

I once taught in an affluent area where most kids were very highly managed. They were "well brought-up," meaning they were enrolled in many extra-curricular activities, their public behaviour was highly prescribed, and they had little unstructured time. One troubling phenomenon among this group was the house party, which many of these kids began to throw around grade 11. At these house parties, there was a kind of anarchy that often resulted in damaging the house. Sometimes the damage would be small, sometimes a major trashing. The other common activities revolved around sex, drugs, and alcohol. In short, there was a complete suspension of the kinds of rules imposed by Mom, Dad, and teachers. The kids involved demonstrated the two kinds of responses to freedom named above. Some kids displayed total passivity — unquestioning acceptance of what's going on. These were not the kids who instigated anything. They simply went along with what was being done. The other response came from the instigators, those who were so pent up, who felt so powerless, who were so eager to assert their will, that they abandoned all limits. These kids would go into a kind of altered state (helped along by drugs and alcohol). They were fighting an invisible foe — all the restraining forces in their lives. Kids who grow up in homes where they experience autonomy and learn self-control generally have much less interest in this kind of behaviour — many even find it irresponsible, disrespectful, and demeaning. They do not have the same need to burn off this pent up need for power and control.

Sometimes the fact that boys spend endless hours on video games is rooted in the same dynamic. They get into the video game, find it completely seductive, and are so passive to its influence that they are not able to exert any kind of personal will to stop playing. The game controls them in the same way that the adults in their lives control them, and they passively — unconsciously — submit to this control. Or they may stay on the game for endless hours as a form of counter-will or rebellion — an expression of personal autonomy. "I do not have any control over my real-world life, but I have total control over my virtual-world life."

Why do most "frosh weeks" (student orientation weeks) at post-secondary schools have such an anarchic tone? Again, there seems to be a deliberate attempt to transgress as many boundaries as possible. During the first week of September 2014, the police department in York region (a suburban area north of Toronto) tweeted a "frosh week expense list," showing the fines for various infractions. The list included things like:

- Urinating on a neighbour's yard
- Forcing a pet to smoke marijuana
- Downing *Jager Bombs* in public
- Shoplifting from a convenience store
- Putting cement mix in a laundry machine
- Smashing bottles on the road
- Starting a fire with your dorm room sofa

One response to the tweet read, "Making it like a checklist seems an awful lot like a challenge." There were similar responses thanking the police for the list — as a prescription for what could be done, not a warning of what not to do. The department used the hashtags #makewisedecisions and #partywithcaution. When adolescents are bent on challenging control in their lives, we only reinforce the dynamic if we tell them what *not* to do. Frosh weeks have become a bizarre North American ritual — whose immense popularity is fuelled by a pervasive parenting style that does not teach self-regulation. Whether it's house parties, video games, school, or frosh week, the dynamic is the same — kids searching for autonomy. They do it in destructive ways because they have so few opportunities to do it in constructive ways. They have not learned self-control because they have seldom been given the chance to practise it.

We hear a lot about helicopter parents, but teachers and schools have been practicing this approach for generations. Children in schools are micromanaged for very practical reasons — crowd control. It is simply a question of the smooth running of the institution. There is no room for individual will in the large group setting. Or is there? I would argue that schools would have less trouble with discipline and classroom management if they taught self-regulation from an early age. And not only taught the concept, but allowed its practice. Kids at school need to be given choices, and they need to understand and feel the consequences of the choices they make. This could most effectively be done in terms of curriculum content — which is highly arbitrary anyway. Let kids choose what they want to study, how they want to study it, to what degree of depth and detail they want to study it, and how they want to demonstrate their learning to the teacher or the class. Another area where students could exercise self-regulation would be in the creation and enforcement of classroom or school policies and procedures. There are some non-negotiable rules in school that must be followed, but there are many "this is just the way we do things" rules that could be discussed and voted upon by students. The whole class loses gym because of the behaviour of one or two kids. Snack time is at ten-thirty, despite kids being hungry by nine-thirty. No one is allowed to go to the washroom until the ten o'clock washroom break. Kids can't bring balls to school because one kid got hit in the head. Running is not allowed in the playground because someone might get hurt. The list of arbitrary rules and regulations in any classroom or school would be a long one. Some are necessary. Many are not. In our society, we have developed democratic institutions to protect us from arbitrary rule. School should be the first and one of the most important places children learn about the principle of democracy, that it is the citizens of a country (classroom or school) who rule and not authority figures with arbitrary laws.

Organized religion can be the ultimate helicopter parent — particularly in the area of morality. Institutional religions, particularly in their most conservative or orthodox forms, encourage obedience over self-regulation. We see the same two responses to organized religion that we see to parents and school — a docile herd that is easily manipulated, or rebellion and complete rejection on the part of those who refuse to be managed. It is no coincidence that rejection of organized religion often occurs in adolescence — a time when the child asserts their will to power. And few ever return to organized religion in adulthood — they continue to refuse what they perceive as a coercive force. It is interesting to note the number of people who reject institutional religion and yet still call themselves spiritual. They still feel the need to respond to a spiritual impulse within themselves. The problem, for them, does not lie in the water the cup holds. It lies in the cup. Sadly, in organized religion the cup seems to have a life of its own, and the welfare of the cup becomes more important than the welfare of those who come to drink from it. Organized religions do not claim to be democratic institutions subject to majority rule. They see themselves as subject to divine rule — which it is their job to interpret and articulate. Responsibility is taught through rules, rewards, and punishments. The person is to be controlled externally. Internal control, self-regulation, and personal responsibility are too unpredictable and too messy. Organized religion, like school and home, would all be more emotionally healthy if more trust was shown and more freedom given.

Self-Monitoring

Self-regulation depends upon self-monitoring. We have to see ourselves in a situation before we can decide how we are going to act in that situation. This might seem like a subtle distinction, but it is an important one — especially when we are part of a group. Research has shown that the larger the group, the less personal responsibility a person takes for their actions. "Everybody was doing it" becomes a logical justification for behaviour within a group. The bigger the group becomes, the less autonomy we feel we have. This has implications for school and the workplace, two common group settings, but the phenomenon also has relevance for those wider groups we are not always aware we are participating in — namely popular culture and cyberspace. The extent to which we practise self-regulation here depends on our ability to self-monitor, to see ourselves as autonomous individuals who are always capable of making individual choices. This lesson begins in the earliest years as we learn self-monitoring.

Very young children see what is going on around them, but they do not see themselves as actors in the drama. In their self-centered universe, all they see are the planets that revolve around their sun; they do not see the sun. During the earliest stages of development this is what psychologists call *phase appropriate* behaviour. Self-consciousness comes later. It also evolves at different rates for different kids. Some children may enter adolescence and still not be aware of how they are coming across. I have worked with fourteen-year-old boys who honestly did not understand why a teacher was angry with them. The boy engages in disruptive behaviour all morning, he is given many warnings, and the teacher loses it around two in the afternoon. "What's your problem?" the boy responds. From his point of view, this is a very sincere question. He has not seen himself in the situation. Children need to be trained in this regard — some more than others. They need to be coached to see themselves as part of the social environment in which they are acting, to see how they are influencing that environment and how it is influencing them. Most children evolve naturally into this awareness. Perhaps some never do. We meet adults who do not seem capable of reading social cues; they are the proverbial bull in a china shop, barrelling through life with no regard for anyone else's feelings or their own impact on others. Whether this is an innate characteristic or the result of poor training remains a question. But when we teach children to self-monitor, by extension we are teaching them to empathize. "What am I doing in the situation?" they learn to ask themselves. "How is what I am doing affecting others? How do others feel?" This is an important series of questions, and children need to be guided along it as they grow. With good intentions, we sometimes tell our children, "it doesn't matter what other people think." We want them to be independent individuals and not follow the crowd. On the other hand, we also want them to have regard for others and to take their feelings into account. It is always a balancing act between what we want and how that might affect others. But before we can self-regulate in this way, we have to learn to self-monitor.

The Rules of the Game

Boys know they need structure and boundaries. They are very aware of their own energy, and they see the need to contain it, manage it, and channel it. One of the reasons many boys are attracted to sports of all kinds is because each one involves the containing and channelling of energy. But playing a sport is not an end in itself. It is done for a purpose — to get the ball in the hoop, the puck in the net, the body to move across the finish line first. Sports are usually goal-oriented, and tend to be presided over by an authority of some kind. No boy begrudges this. In fact, he welcomes it because it implies fairness — justice. There would be much less pleasure in playing a game without rules and boundaries or with no one to ensure that they were being respected.

When we want to understand boys, we always do well to look at what they love and what they willingly accept. If we look at sports, we might find some lessons about disciplining our sons. Discipline is required in sports in order to achieve a goal. So the question arises, what is the goal or purpose of our discipline? Sometimes it is the safety of the child, sometimes it is the safety of others, sometimes it is adherence to a moral code. Mostly, our discipline just has to do with the smooth day-to-day running of the household.

With this in mind, let's name a few questions to ask when it comes to setting rules:

- Does the rule have a reasonable purpose?
- Is the rule easy to understand?
- Is the rule easy to obey?

Here are some simple principles for deciding upon consequences to be imposed for violating those rules:

- Is the consequence humiliating or degrading to the child?
- Is the consequence proportional to the infraction?
- Does the child understand the reasons for the consequence?
- Is the consequence a form of "getting back" at the child?
- Is the consequence a way of burning off our anger?

Adam was playing a video game with his brother in the living room. When he lost, he got mad and kicked the couch. The vibration caused a glass to fall from the china cabinet against the same wall. Adam had all electronics taken away for a month.

My question to Adam's parents is, what rule was broken here? Don't get mad? Don't kick the couch? Don't break glasses? And what was the reason for the consequence?

The event was an accident — it should not have received a disciplinary consequence. It would have, however, been reasonable for Adam to replace the glass. A responsible, self-regulating Adam would offer to pay for the glass without being asked. This is what Coloroso calls *logical consequences*.

Jordan is sixteen years old. His mother knows that he smokes marijuana. She does not approve but has decided she can't control his behaviour outside the home. They agreed on a rule of no smoking marijuana in the house or on the property. One day his mother found a bong for smoking marijuana in his bedroom. (It was an expensive one, a gift from one of his friends). She threw it out.

What rule was broken? What was the reason for the consequence?

No rule was broken. No disciplinary action was required. The mother was expressing her feelings of anger, frustration, and fear about Jordan's marijuana use. Jordan learned only that he must hide his personal life even more from his mother.

The Bubble-Wrapped Child Gets High

In April 2013, the *Globe and Mail* reported the following:

> Teenagers in Canada use cannabis more than any other developed country, according to a new study released by Unicef. The report released last week shows that 28 percent of fifteen-year-olds admitted to having used cannabis in the past year. The figure comes from a World Health Organization (WHO) study conducted in 2009, which surveyed teenagers across 29 developed nations, including more than 15,000 in Canada.

This is the second time in a row that the WHO study has ranked Canadian teenagers as the highest cannabis users, though the percentage of teens itself has dropped. In 2002, the same survey showed that 37.5 percent of fifteen-year-olds in Canada had used cannabis in the past year.

In my own work with teenagers, I have seen a surprising increase in marijuana use. Twenty years ago, the kids I met used marijuana recreationally, mostly on weekends at parties or among small groups of friends. As time went on, I met more and more kids who used marijuana as an after-school activity and then even into the school day — smoking somewhere "off property." What concerns me is the more recent phenomenon of kids smoking marijuana in the morning — for many kids, *every* morning. What is going on here? What is the inner logic in this behaviour? There has been a huge debate in Canada around legalized marijuana for medical use while right under our noses its use for self-medication among teenagers has exploded. We have to ask ourselves the fundamental question: What is the pain teenagers are medicating?

When I ask teenagers this question, I get two main answers: school and parents. In my anecdotal experience, marijuana and alcohol experimentation seems to start around grade ten. It increases in grade eleven, the year a sleeping time bomb goes off in many kids — an inability to cope with the basic challenges of life. They feel helpless and hopeless. They lose whatever sense of personal agency they had. They do not see themselves as strong or powerful. They see themselves as weak and vulnerable. How did this happen? I call it a sleeping time bomb because its roots lie in the past, in the early years — and yes, we must talk again about the micromanaging helicopter parent and the micromanaging school system. The tongue-in-cheek stereotype of the bubble-wrapped generation is true. We made sure our kids wore pads and helmets, but there are no pads and helmets for what they must process and cope with in today's complex world. They were not given the opportunity to learn how to cope with stress and deal with uncertainty at an early age. In other words, they have not developed resilience.

Our parenting and our schooling practices are fear-based. We don't want our kids "going off the rails," so we do everything *we* can to make sure this doesn't happen. Sadly, we end up achieving the opposite result — kids who go off the rails the minute we are not there to manage them. It's no coincidence this often happens in grade eleven — this is the year that house parties begin, friends get their driver's licenses, sex becomes an expectation, and marks begin to count. At this crucial time, parents are no longer welcome. The quest for autonomy and independence is in full swing, and parents can only scream like frustrated coaches from the sidelines. Whatever skills the player has for the game have to have been worked on long ago, and for so many kids, the skills just aren't there.

Parents and teachers need to let kids stand on their own two feet much earlier than they do. More than anything else, we need to show trust. From the very earliest stages, a parent needs to say, "I trust your judgment" — and mean it! People become what they are perceived to be. "You need me to micromanage you because you are basically incapable of running your own life." This is the toxic teaching we pass on through our smothering-loving concern. Kids need to see themselves as powerful and capable. They only learn this by trying and failing and sometimes succeeding. They need to learn responsibility through freedom — through direct experience of the consequences of their actions — not through being constantly told what is appropriate and inappropriate behaviour. Does this mean abandoning our children? Throwing them to the wolves? Not caring? Just the opposite. We throw them to the wolves when we do not prepare them for this incredibly new and complex world. We do not leave. We are there for them — *when they ask!*

5

How We Think About Our Kids

Mindsets: Should I Praise My Child?

As our children grow and demonstrate their abilities, our role is to encourage and affirm them. Our main tool for doing this is praise. Carol Dweck has made an important contribution to this topic in her book *Mindset,* in which she talks about the importance of praising effort instead of ability. She claims there are two main mindsets that people develop: a growth mindset or a fixed mindset. "The growth mindset is based on the belief that your basic qualities are things you can cultivate through your efforts." The fixed mindset believes we are what we are and there is little we can do to change it. The fixed mindset becomes problematic depending on the core beliefs one has about oneself. "I'm basically lazy." "I'm no good at math." These are obviously detrimental thought patterns. But Dweck argues that equally damaging are the core beliefs that can grow from praise such as, "You're special," and "You're smart." Her research found that children who are praised for their ability, for their innate gifts, or for their demonstrated results tend to be more cautious and less willing to develop their skills, and commonly become under-achievers. Rather than have their core beliefs about themselves threatened or disproved, they stop trying.

I have worked with a number of children who were labelled *gifted* at an early age and whose performance began to suffer immediately. In many cases, the child did not go on to achieve their potential, and I believe that Dweck's thesis is right. The child holds himself back out of fear — fear of being exposed as weak, stupid, or incapable. In contrast, she says children who are praised for their effort, for their willingness to face challenges, and for their perseverance are much better off and form a growth mindset. Most of the bright kids I see go on to accomplish impressive things in adulthood do not think of themselves as bright, but they do have a drive to improve. They never lose their curiosity, and most importantly, they are willing to take risks.

Many gifted people who are fed a constant diet of praise develop an inflated sense of their own ability and status. "I am special." "I am different." "I am better than others." "It just comes naturally. I don't need to try hard." Sometimes life will send these kids a *corrective experience*. They will fail in some very public way. At this crossroads the person has an important choice to make. Retreat in fear and never stick their neck out again, or rethink their core ideas about themselves and how they approach life.

Dweck tells the story of a young girl attending her first gymnastics competition. She worked hard to prepare, was encouraged at every turn by her parents, but did not win any ribbons. Dweck proposes five possible ways her parents could respond:

1. Tell her *they* thought she was the best. (Dweck says this is irrelevant and bears no relationship with external reality. It is also insincere because both they and she know she was not the best.)
2. Tell her she was robbed of a ribbon that was rightfully hers. (Teaching her to blame others for her setbacks.)
3. Tell her that gymnastics is not that important. (Teaching her to devalue something if she doesn't do well in it right away.)
4. Tell her she has the ability and will surely win next time. (Dweck says this is the most destructive response because it implies that all you need is ability and success will eventually fall into your lap.)
5. Tell her she didn't deserve to win — yet. (For Dweck, this is the best answer because it's the most realistic.)

She quotes the father's actual response. "Elizabeth, I know how you feel. It's so disappointing to have your hopes up and to perform your best but not to win. But you know, you haven't really earned it yet. There were many girls there who've been in gymnastics longer than you and who've worked a lot harder than you. If this is something you really want, then it's something you'll really have to work for."

Dweck's work is rooted in cognitive behavioural therapy. This method of therapy begins with our thoughts. Many of our problems arise from automatic negative thoughts, which are the product of our core beliefs — about ourselves, about the world, about others. Once these core beliefs are set, they can be very difficult to change. Any kind of labelling, good or bad, can lead to negative consequences. Robert Rosenthal and Lenore Jacobson demonstrated what came to be called *the Pygmalion effect* and *the golem effect*, also known as the *observer-expectancy effect*. The ancient Greek story of Pygmalion tells of a sculptor who fell in love with the statue he had created; the statue, as a result, came to life. He created his own perfect woman. A golem is an ancient character who is the embodiment of stupidity, a slow or dull man formed from clay. Rosenthal and Jacobson found that children who were perceived as more intelligent by teachers performed at a higher level whether they were more intelligent or not. Children who are perceived as less capable become less capable. Children become what they are perceived to be. Some are labelled perfect. Some are labelled flawed. Both situations cause problems.

I have heard many parents describe their child as *lazy* — in front of the child. "If he can avoid doing something, he will." "If there's a quick and easy way to do something, that's how he does it." "Just get it done. That's his way." The reason many kids fall into the "just get it done" approach is because they feel they can't win anyway. If what they do is never good enough, if what they do is always judged, then they will just do the minimum so that those judgments will not be accurate. If they try really hard and fail or are criticized, it hurts, so they just stop trying. Kids turn off not because of constructive criticism, but because of criticism that has no point other than to tear down their attempts. A lot of the criticism or judgment that children receive is not anything they can work with. A child tries really hard on a test or an assignment and gets a grade of C or 65 percent. "What happened to the other 45 percent?" they wonder. "How did I not measure up?" Or as many kids will say, "What did I do wrong?" In video games one does not move on to the next level until one has accomplished all the tasks required of the level they are in. School is not like that. Kids keep moving on to the next task *no matter what their marks are*. So, if those are the rules of the game, why would a child try? They decide to do just enough to get by. Parents and teachers label this behaviour as lazy, but in a way, it makes perfect sense.

Children who do well, on the other hand, have their own internal torment. They wonder when they are going to fall off the tightrope they walk each day. They worry about losing their exalted status. This is especially true for gifted children from whom much is expected. Some rise to the challenge because the bar never really exceeds their ability and so they are safe, but for some, that moment comes when the bar is just a little beyond them. They are exposed as having limits, and they feel a sense of disaster. They stop trying, and settle for good enough.

So what can a parent do?

1. Avoid criticizing. Criticism is not a motivator.
2. Offer constructive criticism with suggestions for improvement, but save them for when the child asks for them.
3. Never label or use language that sums up a person's whole self, like "he's lazy."
4. We should not be embarrassed by our own mistakes or failures, saying things like "how could I be so stupid?" We must model for our children that mistakes and failures are inevitable in life, that we learn from them, correct them, and try to avoid them in the future, but we stay on our path. We don't give up our goals because of them.
5. Convey the message, "You are not your marks. You are not your accomplishments. Your value as a person does not depend on your performance."
6. Avoid talking about the child to other people in front of the child — whether it's praise or criticism. This can make a child feel exposed, and the words we use go deep as a life script. Think of how we would feel if our husband or wife described us to other people in front of us.

Many parents are wounded by their own sense of failure and inadequacy stemming back to their experience of school or their parents' judgments. Consciously or unconsciously, they are determined to change the way the story ends. "I ended up as less than I could have been; my child will not." This is a huge burden to lay on a child, and it is why a parent must come to terms with how they feel about themselves.

Here are some affirmations for parents to say to themselves:

1. My child is not me.
2. My child's success or failure is not my success or failure.
3. I was not a failure.
4. I did the best I could under the circumstances.
5. I am a capable person.
6. My value does not depend on my performance.
7. I am a loveable person just as I am.

Here are some questions for personal reflection:

1. Now that I understand the way in which people become what they are perceived to be, I have to ask myself what did people perceive me to be and was that a fair assessment?
2. If I were to adopt a growth mindset, what skills and interests could I still pursue that I might have given up because I was labelled as not capable and so developed a fixed mindset?
3. Am I comfortable with my own strengths and weaknesses?
4. How do I deal with failure or mistakes in my own life and in front of the children?
5. What are my core beliefs about myself?
6. What are my core beliefs about my child?
7. To what extent do I let my core beliefs about myself influence how I feel about my child?

One of the strongest emotions that can lie behind our parenting is fear. Fear that our child will suffer the same sense of inadequacy that we once felt (and perhaps still feel). Fear that they will not do well financially. Fear that they will end up at the lower end of the social pecking order. We want our children to be confident and able to support themselves comfortably in adulthood (whatever our definition of *comfortably* might be). We undermine these two goals when we let fear rule our lives. Success is the result of effort and resilience. We must praise our children for their work ethic, for their willingness to persevere in the face of adversity, and their willingness to overcome obstacles. We must focus on the character traits that lead to success. Innate ability is not enough. These abilities must be put to use and developed. We are constantly in the process of changing, growing, and developing. We must encourage this in our kids, and, just as importantly, model it ourselves. We can use statements like these:

1. I can't wait to find out who you are.
2. I am always discovering more about who you are.
3. I love who you are.
4. I love who you are becoming.

We should say these four sentences to our children, and then say them to the person in the mirror!

We get what we expect in life — not what we hope for. Our hopes and dreams are often a kind of antidote to our expectations. We hope for the best because we expect the worst. We hope things will go well because we expect they won't. We need to examine our thinking, our view of life. Do we see life as a great adventure full of possibilities opening up at every moment, or do we see our life as a trial to be gotten through, a test to be passed, a burden to be carried? Do we see ourselves as prepared or unprepared for life? Do we see the world as a dangerous place that we must protect ourselves and our children from? These are deep and important questions because they influence the way we act on a daily basis.

Psychologist Elaine Aron said, "If you want to have an exceptional child, you must be willing to have an exceptional child." Most parents do not want an exceptional child. They want an average child. They want a child who will fit in, who will not stick out. They want a child who will be accepted in as many contexts as possible. They want a "normal" child. And yet, we don't have to look far to realize that many successful and accomplished people are precisely those who did not fit in, who were different — and their difference was precisely what made their lives so interesting. The blessing was that either their parents didn't try to hammer those differences out of them or, if they did, the child refused to be turned into something he was not. Why are some parents so open and accepting and supportive of who their children are while others are so fear-based in their parenting? Why do some kids hold on to who they truly are and follow their inner calling while others succumb to the pressures of conformity imposed by parents, school, and peers?

Psychologist Alice Miller, who has written extensively about childhood and parenting, says that children who are resilient in this way, at some point in their lives, would have most likely met an *enlightened witness* — someone who saw them for who they really were. She suggests that such an experience can change the course of a person's life. Many "great" people, when they tell the story of their formative years, will mention a teacher, a grandparent, or someone they met only through books or movies, whom they credit with influencing their direction in life. Many accomplished people will name their parents as the ones who made it all possible, the ones they have to thank. These parents provided the material support but just as importantly the moral support for the *child's own choices*, not the parents' choices. They trusted the child, and followed their lead. They acknowledged to themselves the great mystery of child-rearing — that we don't really know who we are dealing with. Children, like all people, reveal themselves to us in the choices they make, in the things they devote themselves to. We can prune and manage those directions to a certain degree, but ultimately we must let the child be our guide. This attitude requires a huge degree of *trust* in the child, something that is so often lacking. Parents have said to me, "I trust my child. It's the world I don't trust." What they mean is that they don't trust their child to be able to handle the world. What gets passed on is a fear of the world and a victim stance toward it. The dangers and pitfalls of life cannot be denied, but they have to be faced and prepared for. This is our role as parents — to prepare children to face the slings and arrows of outrageous fortune — not to shield them.

What We Do, What We Say, and What We Believe: Not Always the Same Thing

Edgar Schein is one of the world's leading authorities on organizations and how they work. The family is our most basic organization, and much of what he says is relevant to our understanding of it. He shows how what we do, what we say, and what we believe often contradict each other. He calls them *typical behaviours*, *stated values*, and *fundamental assumptions*.

1. Typical Behaviours

Our typical behaviours are the day-to-day things we do and say as we move through life dealing with situations as they arise. They become *typical* when we repeat them in similar situations. They become our way of operating. For the most part, they are unconscious. The more we do them, the less we think about them.

2. Stated Values

Sometimes we slow down enough to stop and actually articulate *why* we do what we do. This usually happens when we feel compelled to justify our day-to-day decisions to our children. At this level, our stated values come to the fore. Our ten-year-old hits our five-year-old. "You don't hit. Everybody deserves respect."

3. Fundamental Assumptions

What lies at the very deepest level (Schein uses the image of the largest part of the iceberg below the water) are our fundamental assumptions. These are unconscious. They are created over the course of our lives and form the program or operating system that influences everything we do and say. This is the level where change has to happen. We have to examine our most fundamental assumptions about ourselves, children, the world, and life. This is, of course, a huge job. These fundamental assumptions were formed by our own childhood experiences, our parents, our cultural background, school, religion, and popular culture. To look at these influences is to become a conscious parent.

The influence works from the bottom up; fundamental assumptions determine our stated values and our typical behaviours. But the influence can go in the other direction as well. By trying out new behaviours and seeing their benefits, by hearing different stated values that sound better than our own, we can modify our fundamental assumptions. Inspirational speaker Richard Rohr said, "We do not think ourselves into new ways of living; we live ourselves into new ways of thinking." We can do both. We need to examine our deepest thinking, and we also need to try out new behaviours.

Let's look at some fundamental assumptions and ask ourselves what influence they might have on our parenting behaviour.

Positive Fundamental Assumptions	Negative Fundamental Assumptions
• Raising kids is fun	• Raising kids is hard work
• Children are basically good and revert to negative behaviour for particular external reasons	• Children are basically bad and need to be coerced to be good through external force
• Emotions make life more enjoyable	• Emotions are scary
• Negative emotions need to faced and dealt with head on	• Negative emotions are bad and should be avoided
• Boys are just as easy to raise as girls	• Boys are more difficult to raise than girls
• Boy energy is a beautiful life force to be celebrated and sometimes managed	• Boy energy is a problem to be solved
• I love being a parent. I'm living in a complicated time. I'm learning and figuring it out as I go along and that's okay because everyone else is too.	• I'm not a good parent. I'm an imposter making it up as I go along hoping no one will criticize me.

Let's look at some possible stated values, and ask ourselves if we live by the positive ones or the negative ones.

Positive Stated Values

These are the kinds of statements one might see or hear in public places. We find them mostly as slogans on letterhead, on website banners, and in speeches by well-meaning dignitaries and politicians.

- Children are our future
- Children are our greatest resource
- Our children come first

- No child left behind

- Success for all
- Excellence in education

Negative Stated Values

We would never come right out and state a negative value. This level of discourse is about our ideal version of ourselves. Nonetheless, there are still some statements that we see as truths that, in fact, limit kids.

- Boys will be boys
- The apple doesn't fall far from the tree
- Spare the rod and spoil the child
- A little spank on the bum now and then never hurt me

Parents can have their own slogans:
- I would do *anything* for my kids
- I just want my child to be happy

Having looked at our fundamental assumptions and our stated values, we must ask ourselves what our typical behaviours actually reveal. We are not what we *say* we are; we are what we *do*. When our behaviour contradicts our core beliefs and stated values, then we have some material to work with in terms of how we could change as parents.

Let's look at some typical behaviours.

Positive Typical Behaviours	Negative Typical Behaviours
• Enjoying our boys — including their squirmy energy	• Judging, condemning, and medicating our boys because of their squirmy energy
• Allowing our children to express the full range of emotions freely	• Stifling emotional expression in our children — especially anger and sadness ("stop crying")
• Focusing on a child's strengths and successes	• Focusing on a child's weaknesses and failures
• Taking care of ourselves and having energy for the kids	• Being constantly exhausted and blaming it on the kids

If we want to take this exercise to an even deeper level, we can look back on the kind of parenting we received. This is important because the way we were parented had a great influence on all three levels of our parenting. What were our parents' fundamental assumptions? What were their stated values? Their typical behaviours? As adults, we are in a position to look back and ask ourselves which were helpful and which ones inhibited our growth. This is not an exercise in passing judgment on our parents. It is an exercise in learning, growing, and evolving. The alternative is simply to repeat the patterns of the past.

Let's take one last look at typical behaviours on a more global level and at how they contradict our stated values. Here we are talking about our behaviour as a society.

Positive Stated Values	Typical Behaviours
• Children are our future	• We are leaving them with the greatest government debt loads in history
• Children are our greatest resource	• We are destroying the environment in which they live

- Our children come first

- No child left behind;
- Success for all;
- Excellence in education

- Children make up the largest group living in poverty
- A small percentage of students achieve the highest levels of academic success measured by marks
- Boys lag behind girls in almost all academic indicators

The Core Beliefs of Institutions

Having looked at our own fundamental assumptions about children and parenting, let's look at some of the fundamental assumptions that underlie the cultures of two very influential organizations — school and religion. School culture affects all kids. Similarly, even if our family does not participate in a particular religious tradition, religions have had a profound influence on our culture. If our children do participate in institutional religion, then we should ask ourselves what some of the core beliefs are even when they are not stated. Whether we are talking about school or religion, institutions have a set of fundamental assumptions that are encoded in their policies and procedures, their rules and regulations. They are even more powerfully encoded in the core beliefs of the people who run them. An institution becomes dysfunctional or toxic when the core beliefs of those who run the institution are dysfunctional or toxic. Our institutions are only as emotionally healthy as the people who run them.

Core Beliefs of School

School is the institution that has the most profound influence on our children, and the emotional environment there is not always beneficial to our boys. Here are some of the core beliefs that can have a detrimental effect on boys' learning, their self-esteem, and their emotional lives generally:

- Boys are more difficult to teach than girls
- Boys are not as well-behaved as girls
- Movement is a problem in the classroom
- Boys are rough

- Boys are impulsive
- Boys are not really interested in learning
- Boys would rather play than learn
- Boys do not pay attention as well as girls
- Boys are lazier than girls
- Feelings matter more to girls than they do to boys
- Boys need to be strictly managed
- Boys cannot be trusted as much as girls can

We have to talk back to these assumptions. We need to undo the bias against boys in our educational system and make schools more boy-friendly. The first step is to educate educators, who are mostly women, about the unique nature of boys — how they communicate, how they learn, and how they behave. The first lesson would be about re-framing boy energy as a positive force and trying to harness it within the structures of school. This would inevitably mean dismantling some of the arbitrary structures of school and revisiting many of its procedures. Most of all, it would mean questioning some of our most fundamental assumptions about students, school, and education. I dealt with these in my book, *What Every Parent Should Know About School.*

Core Beliefs of Religion

Our major religious traditions evolved over hundreds or thousands of years. During this time they accumulated many core beliefs and teachings that are not found in their sacred texts or in the words of their founding leaders. These traditions were influenced by the societies they developed in and the people who encoded them (mostly men). Some of these core beliefs and practices are charming cultural artifacts; others have a toxic effect on the lives of individuals. For example:

- People are inherently bad
- Women are inferior to men
- Women should obey men
- The body is bad
- Sex is bad
- Emotions are inferior to intellect

- Men are prone to temptation — especially sexual temptation
- Self-control is difficult for men
- People need to be controlled by an authority figure (preferably a man)
- Obedience is a virtue
- Punishment is essential
- Those who do not belong to our group are suspect at best, evil at worst

It is easy to see how these core beliefs have come to permeate our culture. They influence our child-rearing practices, our family dynamics, and our educational institutions. They influence our attitudes toward men, women, boys, and girls. They have a profound effect on our emotional health — beginning with the idea that emotions are an inferior function.

6

The Need for Social Engagement

When the fundamental assumptions on which our culture operates are damaging to the emotional well-being of our children, ourselves, and our future, we need to take action. We influence our boys by the way we act with them in the home, but we also influence them by the things we do outside the home, by our social engagement. Our children need to see us acting in the world, taking responsibility as citizens in our local communities and the larger world. Our job is not to create some perfect protective bubble called "our family" where we turn in on ourselves and take care of ourselves — shutting out the world with all of its suffering, cruelty, greed, and hypocrisy. Emotional health includes empathy and a sense of belonging to something larger than oneself. It means having hope for the future because individuals and societies are capable of change — change brought about by the efforts of individuals. We need to teach our children a sense of efficacy, personal power, and personal responsibility for the common good.

So many young people feel powerless about the issues facing our time. When they see their elders — parents, teachers, ministers, politicians — doing nothing, they despair even more. What hope is there in a world without adults? The lack of motivation we see in some kids is partly rooted in a feeling of apathy about life generally. Why bother? No one else is. So many boys are looking for meaning in their lives, especially in later adolescence. A relatively new phenomenon is the *radicalization* of youth in the West, where young people are inspired to travel to the Middle East to fight in religious wars. When we see our boys showing an interest in Islamic jihadist groups, this is symptomatic of a vacuum of meaning in their immediate lives. What do our boys have to be inspired about? What inspiration are we to our boys?

Boys and young men have always been attracted by risk (also called adventure), by fighting (also known as standing up for a cause we believe in — violently or non-violently), and by self-sacrifice (giving ourselves to something we perceive as bigger and more important than ourselves; sacrificing ourselves for the good of others, for the good of society). The question we might ask is what are the battles that need to be fought today? The enemy is not geopolitical. The enemies we face today are racism, sexism, social inequality, and environmental destruction. These enemies cross geographic, religious, and ethnic borders. They are global problems that will require global solutions. Territorial and religious wars are a vestige of previous eras. I believe they will soon burn themselves out as it becomes increasingly clear that we are all in this together. We have one environment, one economy, one human race. How can we inspire our boys to become engaged with those problems that really do threaten our future?

Watching the News

As kids expand beyond the home to the neighbourhood and the town, the next steps are the country and the world. These come to us largely through the news, and the news has become problematic for a number of reasons.

- It emphasizes the negative in the world
- It can be very graphic
- It is everywhere
- The distinction between news and entertainment has been blurred
- The distinction between significant and trivial news has been blurred
- The coverage of complex issues is very superficial

Despite these drawbacks, to be emotionally healthy a child must be aware of his world. As he grows older, he must begin to see that there are social forces at work in the world that have an impact on one's personal autonomy — important things like politics, economics, and law. Feeling helpless in the face of these forces is not conducive to emotional health. An emotionally healthy person sees these forces as things to be understood and managed, and believes that one must become socially engaged, one must act, one must speak up. Voting is the most basic form of social engagement, an external expression to oneself and others that one is aware and involved. The alternative is cynicism and apathy — not indicators of emotional health. At the darkest end of the spectrum are those disengaged young people who feel so powerless and victimized by politics, economics, and law that they take matters into their own hands and commit acts of violence or engage in other socially destructive activities. These are the young people who bring guns into public places or commit simpler acts of vandalism like spray painting "go home" on a mosque. This is not emotionally healthy behaviour. It indicates a feeling of disengagement from social institutions and social norms. It is not just young people we see acting out in these anti-social ways. Parents themselves can become cynical, apathetic, and disengaged as citizens, retreating into their own private world. We need to model working in our communities for the common good. This ideal has been damaged by a media environment that makes individuals feel powerless over larger world events while at the same time encouraging them to find personal empowerment by buying and owning particular products — for themselves.

We can help our children be good consumers of news by finding media outlets that we trust and making the news part of our daily diet of information. This can take the form of print, radio, television, or online sources. Teenagers could be taught to have at least one news outlet bookmarked on their device and to check it daily to keep apprised of world events. We can teach them that this is just something educated people do. Education continues beyond the classroom ar being educated means being socially aware and socially engaged we have come to emphasize education as job preparation, we ha·

the idea of education as preparation to take one's place as a responsible, contributing member of society and to use media as a way to continue learning throughout one's life.

Trauma TV

Since the 1990s, traumatic news stories about things like school shootings and serial killers seem to have increased. When it comes to news, parents must ask themselves whether there is any value in them or their children knowing this particular event happened or knowing its grim details. Many of the most traumatizing news stories can simply be lumped under the heading *socially aberrant behaviour*. Knowing about these events serves no social purpose. Knowing every minute detail serves even less of a social purpose. The journalistic maxim "if it bleeds, it leads" is a sad commentary on the state of our culture. And yet, news organizations trying to attract an audience say that this is what people are drawn to. Kids gather in a circle around a fight. Adults slow down as they pass a car crash. Our interest is piqued by life-threatening situations that do not involve us. They allow us to examine our fear from a distance. We've thought and worried about such things happening to us. We feel a sense of fascination at seeing our worst fears played out and a sense of relief that it is not happening to us. The ancient Greek philosopher Aristotle described this phenomenon as *catharsis*, the arousal of pity and fear for the protagonist leading to a relieving cleansing. We are drawn to crime stories out of pity for the victim combined with fear that it could happen to us — ending in relief when we can turn the channel.

Children do not have enough life experience to need this cathartic experience. For them, watching traumatic events on television is simply traumatic. For them it is not happening at a distance; it is, in a sense, happening to them. Because children have such vivid and active imaginations, they can feel as though they are involved in the events. Children should be protected from detailed coverage of traumatic stories involving human violence or natural disasters. Of course, when a story like the Sandy Hook shootings becomes so well-known that it is talked about in the schoolyard, then we must say something. In such cases, we should take our lead from the child, answering their questions as far as *they* need to take them. We need to impress upon them that these are very rare events. We need to be objective, logical, and sympathetic to all those involved. Lines like "there are some very crazy people out there" are not helpful. Stick to the facts. "A boy became so angry that he decided to hurt other people." The facts can be used as a lesson, but not necessarily directed at the child. We don't want to create a connection in the child's mind between these events and the child's life or personality. Better to generalize and let the child take whatever lessons he needs from the observation. We can say something like "when people get really angry, they need to talk to someone about how they feel. This boy didn't do that. It's important to get help when you're feeling really bad." What is important to realize is that violent crime has decreased dramatically in the past few decades. The reporting of the crimes that do occur has increased dramatically. With the advent of the 24/7 news feed made possible by the internet and social media, we can feel deluged by these events. We need to follow the news, but when the volume of coverage for one event becomes too much, we should just turn it off. News can be informative and educational, but it can also create unreasonable anxiety.

7

Bad Parents

The title of this section raises fundamental questions in parenting. What is a bad parent? What is a good parent? What are the wrong parenting techniques? What are the right parenting techniques? Nowhere does our desire to get it right become more fraught with emotion and more confusing. Is there even a right answer? Perhaps parenting decisions are like chess moves. There is no right chess move. It depends on where all the other pieces are. If we use the term *bad parents*, some parents will worry that they are being described. Others will be interested to hear "those parents" described. Some parents feel insecure and vulnerable to judgment about their parenting. Others seldom question the validity of their approaches. Is parenting a matter of opinion? Is it a matter of faith? Is it solely a topic for psychology? Parenting techniques vary between families, communities, countries, and cultures. Does one group have it more right than another? The great child psychologist Bruno Bettelheim wrote a book called *A Good Enough Parent* in which he said there was no one right way to raise a child. Every child will require a different approach. This complicates the picture even further, but it is an important point. We may not be able to make a to-do list for parenting, but we can perhaps make a "don't do" list. One way to define something is to say what it is not, so we can start to find out what good parenting is by thinking about what bad parenting looks like.

Bad parents don't listen to their kids, but just as importantly they don't listen to themselves. Bad parents are constantly on the lookout for failures, misbehaviour, and other infractions on the part of their children, but they do not monitor their own behaviour in the same way. We talked earlier about self-monitoring and self-regulation. Some people simply do not see themselves in the situation they are in. They see the situation and they see others, but not the role they are playing in creating the situation. We sometimes want to say to someone, "Do you hear yourself?" or "Look at yourself. Do you see yourself?" These are cliché expressions we might use, but in some cases, they are valid questions. Some people cannot hear how they are coming across, and they cannot look at their own behaviour objectively. They are too immersed in it. It is like asking someone to look at their own eyes. We can only see our eyes in a mirror. This is called feedback. Parents are getting feedback all the time from their children's behaviour. Some parents are capable of seeing and hearing it. Others are not. I have worked with many kids for whom the main problem was one or the other of their parents. In my counselling of the parent, the most common line I hear is, "I would do *anything* for my child. I just want him to be happy." And yet, incredibly, I'll discover that the parent's behaviour is the *cause* of the child's unhappiness. So the sentence must be revised to "I would do anything for my child — except change my way of thinking, my way of talking, or my way of behaving." The ability to change one's behaviour in a situation is called self-regulation, but this cannot happen without self-monitoring. We cannot change what we do not see as a problem. More specifically, we cannot change what we don't even *see*.

I am going to go out on a limb and list the behaviours of a bad parent. A bad parent:

- Does not listen. They wait for the child to stop talking so they can say something.
- Does not take the child seriously. "He's just a kid. What does he know?"
- Does not respect the child. "As the adult, I am more important."
- Is inflexible. "My way or the highway."

- Is incapable of changing or modifying their behaviour based on child feedback.
- Puts their own need for power and control ahead of the child's need for autonomy.
- Believes the worst about their child.
- Does not trust their child.
- Automatically believes that their perceptions are more accurate than the child's.
- Rejects the child when the child cannot be controlled.
- Uses criticism to coerce a child.
- Uses humiliation to coerce a child.
- Uses physical pain to coerce a child.

Thinking about *what not to do* as a parent can be as helpful as being told what *to do*.

When Parents Don't Agree About Parenting

Differences in parenting style are usually the result of differences in core beliefs, which we talked about earlier. They are often rooted in the way a person was raised. The parenting style a person experiences becomes their default operating system. The conscious parent looks back on how they were raised, examines what was good and bad about it, and is willing to make changes and try new things. This kind of parent is not as common as we might think. Many parents work on autopilot, doing what was done to them.

The two poles of parenting that most often come into conflict are the strict versus permissive approaches. Does a child need to be highly controlled externally, or given freedom to develop internal controls? Should children demonstrate unquestioning obedience to authority or be listened to and shown respect? When these polarities come into conflict, sometimes the distance is just too far to bridge. Common ground is possible, but it requires huge compromise on both sides. We must decide whether the other spouse's parenting strategies are so negative that the welfare of the children is at stake. If it is, then we have serious choices to make. If it's not, then we might need to step back. A parent has to decide how much energy they are going to invest in this battle, and whether there is any hope of victory. If compromise and change are possible on both sides, then it is certainly worth the investment. If it is going to be a war of attrition over twenty years of child rearing, the toxic effects on the child and the marriage may not be worth it. Sometimes bickering over parenting methods is symptomatic of other cracks in the marriage that have not been attended to, and parenting strategies become the lightning rod for other unresolved hostilities and issues.

Some parents may simply learn to smile at their different approaches and live comfortably with inconsistency. Sometimes the differences in parenting philosophy bother one parent more than the other. Since parenting is so often about power and control, the question can quickly come down to whose strategies are going to hold sway, or, in essence, who is going to be in charge? The two essential elements in the resolution of any power struggle are communication and compromise. Communication does not just mean articulating one's own point of view to another person. It means actively listening to the other person, considering what is valid in their point of view, and looking for common ground with one's own.

Perhaps the fact that Mom and Dad are totally different people and take a totally different approach to parenting will just be the child's story. We cannot change another person, and there are limits to the changes we can inspire another person to make for themselves. The foundation of a committed relationship is love and acceptance. We cannot require other people to be like ourselves. What we may see as a negative or damaging approach may be acceptable (or even positive) to the child. If there is one thing we can be sure about kids, it is that they are incredibly tolerant of adult inconsistency and resilient in the face of adult confusion!

The Foundation Persists

I have worked closely with young people for over thirty years, and have followed many of them through all the developmental stages from childhood to adulthood. There is one truth that I can attest to: the foundation that parents lay down in the earliest years persists throughout life. This has profound implications for parenting. What we do or don't do as parents can alter the course of a child's life. It is a scary and humbling thought, but it should also give us great hope for the future. If we get it right, our kids benefit, and the world benefits. If we get it wrong, a child grows up to be less than he could have been. Getting it right means honouring the nature of the child and creating the optimal conditions for that plant to blossom. The world will soon move in and do its work on the child, but in the earliest years it is his immediate caregivers who will set the trajectory of his life. A child may "go off the rails," particularly in adolescence, but the foundation persists even then. I have seen many kids who were raised with love and respect come out from the chaos of the teen years with their character intact.

Many parents feel so insecure about their parenting that they only remember the mistakes they made, or they focus on their regrets. The second truth that must be added to the idea that the foundation persists is the truth that children are incredibly resilient. They are able to cope with a lot, including our less-than-perfect parenting. Some parents suffer from excessive self-criticism, which is not helpful to anyone. Let's pay attention to the foundation, but let's go easy on ourselves at the same time. There is no such thing as a perfect parent. This is hard for perfectionists to accept.

Part 2
The New Mom and Dad

As women's roles changed, many aspects of their mother role stayed the same. Research shows that women still do the majority of work in the home. We have redefined what it means to be a woman. Now we need to redefine what it means to be a mother and father. Through feminism, the home has reconfigured itself, but not in the same way in every household.

a) Some homes remain a patriarchal environment where Dad has the ultimate say, and Mom and the kids obey. This can be the case even if Mom works outside the home in a position of responsibility or authority. She lives one way at work and another way at home.

b) In other cases, Mom takes charge of the family, and Dad becomes like one of the children. It is a kind of matriarchy. He is left in charge of things like barbecuing and hockey. Popular culture is full of images of the stupid, irresponsible man whose greatest abilities are risk-taking with no regard for consequences. Having fun is his goal, and his wife takes on the role of mother, chastising him for his misbehaviour.

c) In a third scenario, Dad becomes a kind of assistant Mom. He does everything Mom does. He cooks, cleans, does laundry, and cares for the children. From a feminist perspective, this equality in job-sharing is a positive thing as it erases defined gender roles and inequality. This scenario has become the object of mockery in popular culture. The image of the bumbling father taking care of children has grown into a distinct comedy genre, the underlying message being that this is a charming but ultimately doomed enterprise as the father doesn't really have a clue what he is doing. These images and ways of thinking (for one creates the other) make it difficult for men to redefine their role in positive ways.

When the American feminist Gloria Steinem was asked why she finally married at the age of sixty-six, she said she was open to marriage now because marriage had changed so much. She could not have entered into marriage as it was in the 1960s when she says she would have lost most if not all of her civil rights. She was often told that "feminism killed marriage." Her response was, "No, sexual inequality killed marriage. Feminism just exposed it." As feminism changed the roles of women, it inevitably changed marriage. The women's movement reached a critical mass that made it almost impossible for a woman to remain in the old mindset. Women changed, Mom changed, and our expectations about girls changed. In the 1950s and '60s girls were trained for secretarial jobs, teaching, and nursing. They were expected to find a man who could support them while they raised the children.

Today it is taken for granted that all careers are open to girls, and they are expected to become financially independent. Raising children is something one tries to manage around a career. The workload of the new Mom has doubled. She is now expected to be a breadwinner and a homemaker. She is confused and exhausted. If there is one group in our society that needs support, both in emotional terms as well as in practical public-policy terms, it is mothers. We also need to redefine fatherhood so that the nurturing function, previously assigned to mothers only, can be shared more equally.

8

Boys and Their Mothers

It is a fact of nature that females give birth to males. From the female body comes a being very different from her own. It is important for women to understand how boys "work" — how they experience the world, and perhaps most interesting for the mother, how they experience their mother — a story that can only be told from the perspective of males.

A male's experience of his own body and his mother's body begins in the womb — when the two are one. It is an experience of complete harmony and connection. There is no deeper bedrock in our consciousness than the memory of the womb. It is also the place where our relationship to the mother begins. Her experiences, her chemistry, her emotions become ours. We do not have this primal connection to the father. His body is unknown to us. The mother's body is a part of us because we were once part of it.

Just as men can never know what it is to carry and give birth to a child, so women can never know what it is like to not be able to do this, to have been the product of a process but never to experience that process oneself. Women will never know the feeling of disconnection men have from their own children, or to put it more gently, they will never know what it is like not to have the depth of connection that a mother and child have. A father can feel that his child is part of him on a biological and emotional level, but for a mother the connection is much more profound. She walked with this person inside of her for nine months and delivered him into the world with great effort and pain. This creates a connection that no father will ever know. Mothers have said that raising a child is like sending a part of themselves out into the world. On a very material level this is true, and the boy carries his mother with him for the rest of his life. She is in his body, and his deep primordial memory tells him that he was once part of her.

The next most powerful experience of the mother's body that every boy carries is the memory of the breast. One need only look at the profusion of images of the Madonna and Child in Western medieval and renaissance art to know that this is a profound archetype. Archetypes spring from the collective unconscious, said Jung, precisely because they are so powerful in our psyches. The experience of being breastfed is one of the most primal experiences we will ever have — to feed from the body of another.

Apart from its dietary benefits, breastfeeding is important for bonding and attachment. There has been much research in the past few decades on the importance of attachment in child development. Research shows that a strong bonding and attachment to a primary caregiver is an essential factor in preventing future issues with cognitive functioning, emotional well-being, and even physical health. Breastfeeding is one of the most powerful ways in which this bonding and attachment occurs.

For boys, the experience of the mother's body in the womb and at the breast has a bearing on our relationship to the natural environment. We use the metaphor of *mother earth* for good reason. The earth sustains us in the same way a mother's body sustains her child both in the womb and beyond birth. Most children growing up in the past several decades have not had the degree of attachment to mother that previous generations did, nor do they have the same degree of exposure to nature. This must have implications for child development. Is our growing disregard for mother earth the result of less contact with mother and less contact with the earth? The great evolutionary biologist Edward O. Wilson coined the term *biophilia* — love of life, or a desire to connect to other life forms. Does this love begin at the breast? Is the mother's body the matrix that establishes this love? Whether it's the desire to hold a baby, hug a child, plant a garden, stroke a pet, or even to travel to other planets, we all seek connection with other life forms. If our first attachment is blocked, interrupted, or conflicted, will this affect a child's later development and their relationship to the natural world? Our growing disconnection from the earth, our apparent indifference to it, may be connected to our disconnection from our mother's bodies as well as our own bodies. One way to improve or protect emotional health may be through reconnection to mother earth. If author Richard Louv's thesis is correct, we are suffering from "nature deficit disorder" and the solution is to reconnect with our first and most important mother — the earth.

With the fundamental changes in women's roles in society has come a profound conflict — mostly felt by mothers — between the demands of the workplace and the demands of motherhood. We have changed the rules about who can work, but we have not done enough to change the rules about how we work. There is little accommodation for the needs of mothers (or fathers) in the workplace. Productivity and parenting are incompatible in the business world.

One morning Julia's one-and-a-half-year-old son woke up with a high fever. She had a contract position with a movie production company and had to make a decision whether to call in sick or not. Her partner was out of town. She was torn between the needs of her baby and the economic need to be seen as a reliable employee — someone who would be there consistently and give her full attention to the job. Unfortunately, this definition of a good employee is also a fair description of the role of parent. After much tormented soul-searching (which had to be done quickly), she made the decision to call in sick and stay home with her baby. She told me how she lay with him on her chest most of the day, how beautiful the experience was, how bonding. She did not regret her decision at all, but it bothered her that she even had to make it in the first place.

We are not a child-friendly culture. We are not a parenting-friendly culture. Children and the demands of parenting are seen as inconveniences, as unproductive, as obstacles to the efficient running of the marketplace. And, for the most part, it is mothers who are made to feel guilty about the demands of parenting and the impositions caused by children. We do little in our culture to support mothers. Mothers just have to make do. We do not consider the resulting stress for the mother or the child. We do not consider the implications for bonding and attachment. We impose an economic yardstick first and emotional considerations are seen as dispensable or even frivolous. Raising emotionally healthy children will mean creating social and economic policies for parents that support it.

Separation from Mother: Too Fast? Too Slow?

If the primary attachment to mother is the most important bond for a young boy, then one of the most significant events in his life will be his separation from his mother. This separation does not just happen once but several times in a boy's life — at birth, in childhood, at puberty, with marriage, and with the death of the mother. The first experiences of separation are the most profound, and have implications for the future trajectory of a boy's life. Separation from the mother, a willingness to venture out on one's own, to be independent, to try out one's skills in the world, is an exhilarating and necessary step that all boys must take. The questions become when and how is this to be accomplished? For every boy the timing is different.

Some boys remain strongly attached to their mother longer than others. They are variously described as *mama's boys* or as *clingy*. But these boys just have a different threshold of tolerance for the kind of stimulation separation from the mother inevitably brings. They are on their own developmental timeline. We would never pull a half-formed butterfly out of its chrysalis. We would never take a tadpole out of the water and force it to hop. But we do these kinds of things all the time with children. We just can't see the distress — or do we see it but ignore it? As so often happens, we assume that all children of a certain age are the same. We impose adult conceptions of what a child *should be* on what our children *actually are*. We ignore their nature. Apples on the tree do not all fall from their branches at the same time. Some apples fall early, others later. We don't give that reality a second thought. We need to adopt a similar organic attitude about children at all their developmental milestones, perhaps most importantly the milestones that involve separation from the mother. When we see separation anxiety, we take it as a problem to be solved, a disorder, a dysfunction. But for that child, it is an appropriate response to his experience. We all see

reality differently. We all have different levels of tolerance for stimulation and change. We need to be aware of these differences in our
children. If a child is forced prematurely into extended periods of separation from his mother, these experiences may make him distrustful
and overly cautious. "It was so hard the first time," he thinks. "It will
always be hard." And even when it becomes easier, he thinks, "I still remember how hard that was, and I don't want to have that feeling again."

We sometimes push our children toward growth. We want to help
them expand their horizons of experience and their repertoire of behaviours. We push them with good intentions, but sometimes there is
a social pressure to push them in ways that we know intuitively they are
not ready for. We act out of fear — fear of my child being weak, unable
to cope, or left behind. It takes a strong parent to resist these social pressures to "get your child in the game as soon as possible." Many parents
speak proudly of how easily their child adapts to new situations, or how
quickly they are able to initiate play and conversation with children they
hardly know. Why do we see this as such a positive thing? Because these
behaviours are necessary for survival in a culture that does not tolerate
different temperaments, that moves very fast and requires quick assimilation into unpredictable environments. Everyone must get with the program as soon as possible. This is how one makes it in this world — by
fitting in. For some children, particularly highly sensitive children, this
approach can be harmful to their emotional health.

Psychiatrists Alexander Thomas and Stella Chess devised nine
categories of temperament in children. These categories can help us
understand our child's nature by describing their innate ways of relating to the world. Having language to describe our children's behaviour
can be very helpful in interpreting it and knowing how to react to it. A
child's temperament can be described in terms of where they fall along
a spectrum for any one of these attributes. For example, a child may
have a high, average or low activity level.

1.   Activity: the level and extent of motor activity;
2.   Regularity: the rhythmicity, or degree of regularity, of
     functions such as eating, eliminating, and sleeping;

3. Approach or withdrawal: the response to a new object or person, in terms of whether the child accepts the new experience or withdraws from it;

4. Adaptability: the adaptability of behavior to changes in the environment;

5. Sensitivity: the threshold, or sensitivity, to stimuli;

6. Intensity: the intensity, or energy level, of responses;

7. Mood: the child's general mood or disposition, whether cheerful or given to crying, pleasant or cranky, friendly or unfriendly;

8. Distractibility: the degree of the child's distractibility from what he is doing;

9. Persistence and attention span: the span of the child's attention and his persistence in an activity.

Four of these categories have a direct impact on how a child experiences separation from the mother: approach or withdrawal, adaptability, sensitivity, and intensity. When we respect the nature and boundaries of our child's nature, that child grows up to be stronger, not weaker. Children need to feel that their primary caregivers understand them and empathize with them, and this is not just communicated through words. It is communicated by our actions. If a child is fearful in a situation and needs to be close to Mom or Dad, to be held or have his hand held, that is okay. It is interesting to note how *holding someone's hand* has become a kind of pejorative expression. "He needs to have his hand held" is a statement about weakness. "You can't hold his hand all the time." It's like that other expression (which conjures up an outdated image) *cutting the apron strings*. Dependence on the mother is immediately feared to be over-dependence. Many mothers express concern about their clingy child. My advice, as always, is to take your lead from the child. All behaviour is logical. If our child has an emotional need, our job is to meet that need. The word need is important in this context. We see the need as a want. On the surface, it may appear to be a superficial want. But there is a fundamental difference between "I want that candy" and "I want to be held." The first one is not a need

— no child needs candy. The second has to be respected as a need or interpreted for the message that it is. The message might be "I'm afraid," "I'm tired," "I'm confused," or "I'm overwhelmed." And, yes, it might be, "I know I should try this new situation, and it's not really that scary, but it's easier to hold onto you and avoid it." This is where our wisdom comes in and our knowledge of the whole child and their temperament. We fear raising a "spoiled" child — one whose every whim is indulged. If we know and respect our child, then we need not fear spoiling him. What we really fear is being taken advantage of, of appearing like a pushover. Like so many parenting decisions, the decision about how to respond to one's child in a particular situation is often as much about us and how we will appear to others as it is about the needs of the child. It also becomes, once again, a question of power and control. "Am I controlling my child or is my child controlling me?" If a parent is confident in their adult role, they do not worry about the child "taking over."

One of the biggest struggles in any boy's life is the struggle to achieve autonomy and independence. The counterforce to this goal is the sometimes equally strong pull toward dependency. When a rocket is leaving the earth, it needs a huge amount of thrust in order to break free of the earth's gravitational field. Once it is in outer space, a rocket requires very little energy to move. A similar dynamic happens in every boy's life. The clingy boy is simply not ready for this project yet. He is gathering strength for his personal take off, which will inevitably come to pass, but every boy has his own time when this will feel right. One of the voices that comes into this struggle is the voice of shame: "Be a man!" "Don't be such a baby!" Every boy knows this voice, the tough-guy stance. Some boys will put this persona on like a poorly fitting suit. They pretend they can handle it. They pretend they are enjoying it — because that's what is expected. It is an act, and sometimes too much of the self is denied in the process.

Should every boy be held close as long as possible? Every boy has his own threshold for when he's ready to step out on his own. We can err by pushing him out there too soon, and we can also err by waiting too long. A boy needs to test himself and prove himself. He needs to gradually expand his horizons by stepping outside his comfort zone.

Mother's arms are the natural place of retreat when the going gets too tough, but he must venture out again once he has been restored. It is a process, not a one-time event. It happens in increments. Eight-year-old Matthew went kicking and screaming to swimming lessons. He was highly sensitive and deathly afraid of the water. His parents thought this would be the way to help him overcome his fear. He was forced to stay through ten sessions. He did the absolute minimum required, and ended the sessions still in the beginner level he started at. He was humiliated, still afraid, and avoided the water even more for the next ten years. During high school, pool parties were a trial to be gotten through by pretending he had forgotten his bathing suit or just wasn't interested in swimming. One summer during university he worked at a resort where he asked the life guard if she would teach him to swim. He took to it quickly for a number of reasons — he was ready, there was no one judging him, and it was his decision, not someone else's.

Because the mother has had such an intimate relationship with the child over many years, there is a natural desire to continue to hold the child close. The mother bear guarding her cubs, the duck waddling with a row of ducklings behind her. These images resonate with us because we are a species that cares for its young for an extended period of time. Mothers can be naturally reluctant to abandon this vital role — especially in a world that is not always very kind. This is where the father can play an important role. He will often be a kind of bridge between the protective, sheltered world of the mother and the challenges of the external world. The father is generally more comfortable in this boundary-pushing, horizon-expanding role. The downside of this scenario is that Dad can get cast in the role of adventurous risk-taker while Mom gets cast in the role of cautious worrier. Sometimes Mom must be the one pushing her son out the door.

Failure to Launch

The stereotype of the unemployed or under-employed twenty-something living in his parents' basement playing video games is a valid concern. The statistics on the prevalence of this phenomenon are disturbing. Part of the cause is economic, but there is a parenting dimension as well. We need to hold our kids close, but we need to teach them resilience and autonomy at the same time. It is not an either/or situation. As parents we oscillate back and forth between pushing and holding, but we cannot hold onto the back of the bicycle seat forever. Eventually we have to let go. We fear their falling, but it is inevitable. We comfort them when they fall, but they must get back on the bike and try again.

Where is the line between respecting a child's need to be held close and becoming an over-protective helicopter parent? Peter is fifteen years old and lives about a five-minute walk from my office. His mother will sometimes call to cancel Peter's appointment because she is not able to drive him. Matthew's mother does his homework for him while he plays video games. Sixteen-year-old Aidan has never ridden on a city bus alone. Ben in grade ten has never bought his own clothes. Mom buys them; he tries them on at home, and she returns what he doesn't like. Dylan is in his second year of university and has never had a part-time job in his life. These boys have not been well-served. Their emotional development has been arrested by holding off too long on the essential process of letting go.

There are several criteria we can apply when deciding whether it's time to hold close or time to let go:

- Take your lead from the child
- Know the child's temperament
- Never let fear rule your decision
- Assume an attitude of trust toward the child
- Trust your intuition
- Adopt the assumption: "You are strong and capable. You can handle this"
- Mothers — trust Dad's point of view
- Fathers — trust Mom's point of view
- Don't let the opinions of in-laws, siblings, or neighbours cloud your vision

Failure-to-launch is another way of describing the problem of the uninitiated male. We say that girls *become* women but boys are *made* into men. When a girl reaches puberty, a biological imperative sets in and she becomes even more like her mother. There is a continuum in the mother-daughter relationship that does not exist for boys. When a boy reaches puberty, he becomes something quite different from his mother. This fundamental fact goes largely unacknowledged in our culture. We have no initiation rituals; in fact, we don't even talk about this. Boys are left on their own to figure it out. They can end up very confused, and sometimes we see them trying to initiate each other — in all kinds of awkward and destructive ways. What boys need are men, fathers, who take on this vital role of initiating boys into positive manhood. The problem is that many men still feel like uninitiated boys themselves. Ever since the traditional construction of masculinity fell apart in the 1960s, the question for males has been "initiation into what?" If I do initiate my son, what do I initiate him into? What did it used to mean to be a man? What kind of masculinity was I initiated into? What could it mean in the future?

9

Redefining Fatherhood by Redefining Manhood

Any attempt to redefine what it means to be a father will require a redefinition of what it means to be a man.

- He has his own set of values and shares these with his children
- He is seen acting according to these values
- He reflects on his experience and is open to learning from his experience
- He takes responsibility for his commitments (marriage, children, and job)
- He is socially engaged
- He models respect for all women
- He models respect for all people (including those of different races, cultures, and creeds)
- He puts relationships ahead of material possessions
- He spends time with his wife
- He spends time with his children
- He pursues his own interests
- He is connected to the natural world and leads his children there
- He pays attention to his own elders and passes on what has value
- He prepares to become an elder himself someday
- He laughs and has fun
- He takes care of his own health
- He is affectionate

- He is comfortable in his own body
- He is comfortable with the bodies of his children
- He enjoys nurturing touch

Male Energy

There is such a phenomenon as male energy (just as there is female energy). The burgeoning male energy in a boy is drawn out through resonance with the male energy of a man. At the same time, a man's male energy is stimulated and strengthened by contact with male youth. Men and boys communicate differently when they are with each other than they do when women or girls are present. Also, when an individual man and boy are together, they communicate very differently than they would if other males were present. There is no sense of competition, or at least there should not be, since the man has a natural advantage due to his age, strength, and experience. He must respect where the boy is at that moment, acknowledging what he is capable of at the current stage in his development. Empathy plays a large role in this, the man putting himself in the boy's shoes, remembering what it was like to be a boy himself. Men show boys how to be men. Boys learn how to be men by being with men. There are not enough positive opportunities for this in our culture.

As mentioned earlier, fathers can play the role of bridge between the mother-child world and the larger world. This is not to say that mothers cannot play this role too. Of course they can, and they do. In early childhood in particular, mother will often be the facilitator of those first moments of independence. As the child grows older, and particularly in early adolescence, Dad comes to play a unique role in a boy's life — guiding him into new territory. This will inevitably entail spending more time together, which is a huge part of the process. As father becomes the guide and facilitator of new experiences, the boy learns who Dad is in a way he could not experience in any other way. It is felt on a deep, existential level. It is usually non-verbal. It happens through the alchemy of being together, doing things together, and, yes, some talking — but the talking is almost a distraction from the real process that is going on unseen below the surface.

I once went on a backwoods camping trip with one of my sons and another father and his son. We canoed and camped along the coast of Georgian Bay for about four days. When we returned to the boat-launch area, there were several groups just getting ready to leave. What shocked me was how much talking was going on among them — incessant chatter about every detail concerning their launch. Our group paddled up to the dock and began the process of unloading, which had now become routine — our visual-spatial brains had taken over from our verbal brains. We worked in unison with hardly any talking at all. It was as though we had reverted to some more primitive way of being, back to our original nature. The male brain is predominantly a visual-spatial brain. It has learned to become verbal. When males are alone together, they do not talk as much as women do, but that does not mean they are not communicating. Male identity, like male energy, is transferred through physical proximity, action, and words. Boys need fathers, or other significant males in their lives, to spend time with them doing things. This is how boys learn to be men.

Boys in Groups

We need to distinguish between the kind of male energy that exists between a man and a boy alone and the male energy that arises in groups of males. Typical boy group situations include:

- A group of ten-year-old boys at a birthday party
- A group of seventeen-year-old boys celebrating a sports victory in a locker room
- A group of young men at a stag party
- A group of young men playing video games online

In all of these situations, we can picture loud, aggressive, posturing behaviours. The topic of male energy has become a difficult one in our culture because the kind of male energy that emerges in groups of males is not always positive. When numbers increase and there is no age-mixing, males generally seek to establish a pecking order and achieve dominance in the group. The process for making this happen can become pretty noisy, rough, and sometimes cruel. In the scenarios above, one of the common elements is that each is an "unstable" group — a group with no history, no structure, no leadership, and therefore no established pecking order. Boys do best in groupings that are "stable," either because they have a substantial history in which roles and status have become defined, or the group has a built-in structure that assigns roles and confers status (in a legitimate way). Many boys today suffer from the stress of constantly finding themselves in unstable groups where they are never really sure where they stand. Boys find themselves in a large array of groupings from a very early age: daycare centers, after-school programs, sports teams, camps of all types — tennis camp, golf camp, art camp, drama camp. These ventures are well-meaning, and certainly play a practical role in the busy lives of parents, but what boys need at some point is an environment that is stable, predictable, has a history, has rituals, and in the best-case scenario has age-mixing, including the presence of men.

In Canada, hockey is one of the most common groups boys find themselves in outside of school. They are drawn to hockey (and other sports) because it meets many of the criteria listed above. The rules are clear and predictable. There are certain rituals, and some teams even have a history. The boys are usually within an age range of about two or three years, so there is some sense of ascendancy by size and age. What has become controversial in the past few years is the quality of male leadership in hockey. Men with a broad range of philosophies, styles, personalities, and techniques start out coaching hockey, but many drop out, disenchanted with the culture they find there. By the mid-teenage years, team coaches who have stayed tend to adhere to a particular set of values and match a particular profile. It would be wrong to paint all coaches with the same brush, but having taught and counselled hundreds of Canadian boys who loved playing hockey, I have been saddened by the stories they tell and the reasons many of them give for eventually abandoning the game they love. Bullying, criticism, ridicule, retaliation, condoning of violence, the drive to win at all costs, insensitivity, and arrogance are just a few of the behaviours they report seeing in the locker room, on the ice, and in the stands. These cultures are created, condoned, and encouraged by adults who are responsible for leading boys to manhood. More needs to be done in this hugely popular male sport — and other sports with similar issues — to consciously work on creating a positive, supportive culture. Boys are socialized by the groups they belong to. We need to pay closer attention to the variety of groups available to boys and their quality.

It is hard to think of scenarios in our culture where groups of males can come together in other ways. It is also hard to think of situations where males of various ages would come together. Why is this the case? Sports has become the last male preserve. It is the only place left in our culture where we tolerate gender segregation. There are few places for men to come together in socially constructive or personally constructive ways that are *exclusively* male. Women's fitness clubs, women's book clubs, women's business associations, Moms groups, female networking groups of all kinds have proliferated. Men do not connect like this in meaningful ways. Some would argue that men don't need to connect because the world is one big old boys' club, but that old truth is fading away. Men do not spend time together in ways that are personally, intellectually, or spiritually strengthening. Physical strength is the only thing men allow themselves to work on together in the same room. Many men feel lonely and isolated. Their primary emotional support comes from their wives. It will be hard to foster any kind of "men's movement" because, outside of sports, men don't come together. Consciousness raising is unlikely to happen in the sports arena as only a limited part of what it means to be a man is celebrated (or permitted) there.

The Emotionally Absent Father

We cannot speak of *the role of the father* as a monolithic idea. History shows us that fathers have played different roles during various periods in history and anthropology shows us that fathers continue to play various roles in different cultures. In the industrialized cultures of the West, fathers have been significantly separated from their children since the Industrial Revolution. When men became cogs in the machinery of industrial capitalism, there was little left of them for their children. Father hunger is a deep wound in our culture. It has been for the past three hundred years, but is felt more strongly now because of raised expectations for what a father should be. When father was absent in the nineteenth and early twentieth century, this was part of his noble duty as provider for the family. His absence was a sign of merit. Children hardly knew their fathers, but loved them from a distance. This was simply a cultural norm, and whatever pain it caused was lessened by social convention. Many older men do not spend a lot of time lamenting the absence of their father. "That's just how it was back then," they say. As gender roles have shifted, expectations have shifted. Men are expected to be emotionally present, and they feel guilty about not being able to live up to these expectations.

When a man is emotionally healthy, he is able to be emotionally present. The emotionally absent father is a man cut off from his own emotional life. Here we are at the root of the problem in men's lives generally. They do not *have* their feelings. They put them away, repress them, swallow them — whatever the language is that could describe such a complex phenomenon. Their feelings are put away by choice and by compulsion. There are internal pressures at work as well as external pressures. "I have work to do. I have to earn my status in the group. I have to prove myself to others. People are expecting things from me, and I have to produce. I have to perform. There is not time or space for feelings. Having my emotions is just too much to handle. Having my emotions is just too messy. I don't have the time or the energy for this."

Men are trapped in cages of their own making. What we are slowly coming to discover is that the cage door is not locked. We don't need to live like this. Our hope lies in the younger generation of fathers who have not become as entrenched in their behaviour, who have not yet copied their fathers, who are willing to experiment with new ways of being a man. If we raise emotionally healthy boys, we will create more of these men in the future and then our definitions of masculinity and fatherhood will change even more and we can create a cycle of growth. Healthier boys become healthier men, but boys need healthy men to show them the way. This is the paradox, the Catch-22 situation. When men are cut off from their emotional lives, they are, in turn, cut off from their children. They are not able to express their love spontaneously and fully. It is a wound many men feel and, needless to say, many children feel it as well. Men stand to gain what women have never lost — close connection with their children.

Looking Back at Our Own Fathers

Many fathers feel incompetent because they don't have role models to follow. However poor or limited our own fathers were, we can still learn much from them. If we look deeply into our own fathers' lives, if we pull back the mask, we will be able to see their humanity, their vulnerability. The most powerful scene in the whole *Star Wars* series, some would say the climax, is the moment when Luke Skywalker removes the mask from his father, Darth Vader. The whole *Star Wars* story turns out to have two plots — the defeat of the dark forces of the Empire and Luke's quest to discover who his father is. The two stories are not unrelated. The "forces of darkness" are very real in a man's life, and one of the ways he overcomes them is by discovering who he truly is. A big part of this quest involves going back to the father, to the ancestors. "Who am I?" raises the questions "who was my father?" and "who were my ancestors?" I've known many men who became interested in genealogy in middle-age. The Buddhist monk Thich Nhat Han goes even deeper. He says we carry our fathers within us. This is true both on the level of DNA and on a spiritual and existential level. We carry the unlived lives of our ancestors and we carry their unresolved pain, but if we go deep enough, we also carry their wisdom.

My own father was a very quiet man, a perfect example of the emotionally absent father. I understand now that he was highly sensitive, extremely introverted, and a slow language processor. He was traumatized in his own childhood, and carried an ancestry of unresolved trauma. He sat silently at the dinner table partly because there was just so much talking and activity going on with five kids spread over a thirteen-year age range. I am sure he was overwhelmed by it all. My mother was very verbal and extroverted and presided over the dinner table with many words and a strong authoritative presence. My father was a travelling salesman who lived out of his car. I once heard Richard Rohr talking about men and prayer, and he suggested that for many men, their car is their monastic cell, the place where they do their best thinking and feel most at peace. This really struck me, and I'm sure that's what my Dad's car was for him. He would leave early on Monday morning before we left for school and would not return until Friday night around dinner time. Over the course of the weekend he wouldn't say much. Our TV was always on, but Dad would hardly watch it at all. He would sit in the living room and read or work downstairs in his makeshift office going over his accounts of the past week and preparing for the week ahead. Going to church on Sunday was the family's main social experience. Then on Monday he was gone again. There was never any playing with Dad or talking to Dad. He was just this quiet male presence lurking on the periphery of my boyhood and adolescent consciousness.

In adulthood, I did the work that many men find themselves compelled to do — to go back and try to lift the mask from the father's face, to look beneath the surface of behaviours and perhaps ask some difficult questions. Dad had never talked about his own extended family or his childhood. When I finally asked him for the details when he was seventy, he was surprisingly willing to share his story. It almost seemed like a relief to him. His mother died of asthma a few days after giving birth to him at their house in Battle Creek, Michigan, in 1915. His mother's sister came from Ontario and took the baby home to care for. Two years later, his father remarried and came to claim the toddler — a move that was very traumatic for the family who now loved Bernie as one of their own. He was raised by his alcoholic father and a stern Seventh-Day Adventist step-mother who moved from town to town in upstate New York and Michigan trying various business enterprises. The only constant that kept them out of the poor house was his father's ability to fix Singer sewing machines. This he did in many places and seems to have passed some of that knowledge on to my father who was always able to fix my mother's sewing machine. (My father was not handy at all, and this ability always struck me as mysterious and strange.) As an early adolescent my father spent a couple of years at a Christian Brothers school in Windsor. Then the depression hit and the family came back to a meager existence near Kitchener living with estranged relatives and working odd jobs. Dad talked about stealing eggs and sucking them for something to eat. His first real job was in the Hespler textile mills, but the sound of the machines was so loud he had to quit. His next adventure was the Canadian Army, with the Royal Hamilton Light Infantry. He was sent to England, and at the training camp in Aldershot, his nature caught up with him. Preparations began for the disastrous raid on Dieppe, and on one of his leaves, he met a young woman in London who was an artist. She led a bohemian existence and introduced Dad to art and sex. This was all too much for the boy from rural Ontario, and he ended up having what was referred to in those days as a nervous breakdown. He was hospitalized, and in the hospital he was introduced to oil painting as part of his therapy. His mother had painted, and he discovered he had a talent for it as well. He was given an honourable discharge and sent back to Toronto where he got a job in the John Inglis armament factory and met my mother. In the home I grew up in, a beautiful oil painting of a bridge hung on the living room wall; we kept a mountain scene with an American eagle on a shelf in the fruit cellar. These paintings were just there. They were never spoken of; their origin was never explained. I never saw him paint or draw. This was all part of another life, another self that, like so many men, he had to put away in order to get on with the practical demands of life.

My father's story is similar to many men's lives. A man of a particular nature thrust into circumstances for which he is not completely ready — coping, camouflaging, surviving — and then one day breaking down — overcome with feelings of being unprepared and unable to cope. This is usually followed by some kind of course correction, which is often one with diminished horizons, a "settling for." Men adopt the motto "I'm never going to let that happen again." They learn to play it safe. They learn to protect themselves, but they always remember the glimpse they had of their own personal truth — the reality of who they are underneath it all — and that vision haunts them for the rest of their lives. For some boys and men, this moment of breaking or exposure may be very mundane. A public humiliation, a failure at some highly invested activity, or rejection by another. For others, it might be a very dramatic and public fall. The myth of Icarus is a powerful male story. Daedalus the master craftsman, the capable father, makes a pair of wax wings for his overly-enthusiastic son, Icarus, who wants to push beyond his limits and prove himself. His father warns him not to fly too close to the sun, but Icarus, in his hubris, ignores the caution. The wax wings melt under the heat, and Icarus falls to his death in the sea. Many men have had their heated moment of trial and fallen into the sea. No man ever forgets this.

My father never spoke of his childhood, his own father, or his experience in the war. He felt shame about all three. Reading more deeply into my father's life, I see how misplaced these feelings were. His childhood was marred by his mother's death, his father's alcoholism, and the Great Depression, none of which he had any control over. The Second World War scarred him in the way it scarred thousands, not with bullet wounds but with emotional ones. In our narratives of war, we never hear about the men who did not want to be there, the men who were scared to death and turned and ran in the other direction — away from the madness.

Part of the feminist project has been going back into the past to look at the lives of women who never achieved their potential, who were held back by economic and social structures. Feminists inevitably thought about their own mothers, their grandmothers, and women going back centuries. They found women who were trapped, who suffered unquestioningly, but they also looked for and found proto-feminists, early examples of women who had thrown off social norms, who lived a kind of freedom despite external constraints. Men need to engage in a similar project. We need to look at our fathers, our grandfathers, and all the men who lived "lives of quiet desperation" to use Thoreau's phrase, men who laboured under the yoke of patriarchy, industrialization, and capitalism — all those social arrangements that deformed the minds and hearts of men.

We talk about patriarchy, industrialization, and capitalism as things that benefited men and excluded women. While it is true that these systems excluded women, it would be wrong to say they benefited men. They benefited a *few* men. The rest were left feeling like failed versions of the successful ones. This is best illustrated in the classic American play *Death of a Salesman*. The main character, Willy Loman, cannot understand how his brother, Ben, did it. "When I was seventeen I walked into the jungle, and when I was twenty-one I walked out. And by God I was rich." Willy is always trying to figure out what the secret is. He can only guess that it has something to do with being "well-liked." He has devoted his whole life to the American Dream, and it has failed him. Some analysts have suggested that there is no class envy or class conflict in the United States because of the common belief that anyone can be a millionaire through determination and hard work. The poor do not begrudge the wealthy their wealth because they see it as a natural result of this dream. They see themselves as failed millionaires who may one day still make it — or perhaps their children will. There is no tolerance for talk of root causes or systemic injustice. Those are difficult abstractions too complex to analyze. Better to just buy into the dream. This is what men in the West have been doing for the past three hundred years. The American Dream is a variation on the Protestant Work Ethic — the idea that God rewards those who work hard, and wealth is a sign of God's favour, indeed of a person's virtue. The flip side of this is not very encouraging for those who are not rich.

As women unearthed a feminist tradition going back centuries, men need to find the same lineage. All through history there have been men who questioned the roles they were assigned and questioned the systems that kept people locked in these roles. Henry David Thoreau was a nineteenth-century writer who left society in order to see it more clearly. He lived for two years in a cabin near Concord, Massachusetts, where he kept a journal recording his observations and reflections about society. His brief essay "On the Need for Civil Disobedience" became an important inspiration to the work of Mahatma Ghandi and Martin Luther King. We might eventually begin to see a lineage — ancestors, men, who refused to participate in systems that compromised their own integrity, or as educator and activist Parker Palmer put it, "refused to be complicit in their own diminishment." One of our problems is we don't have a name for these men. The word *masculinists* doesn't quite work. The phrase used by historians tracing the history of male accomplishment has always been "Great Men of History." This usually means kings, politicians, and military leaders. These were all men who worked within the system, steered the ship of state, and did not rock the boat. We need to recover the stories of those who got off the ship and set out on their own in boats of their own making — looking for new lands, new ways of being, new rules. One of the ways we can spot these men is by the fact that they were either seen as failures in their own lifetimes or not paid much attention to at all. In many cases they were actively shunned and rejected by their contemporaries.

The Land of Our Fathers: Immigration Trauma

I grew up and spent my teaching career in and around the Toronto area — one of the most multi-cultural regions in the world. As a student in the sixties and seventies I was surrounded by Italian immigrants; in my first teaching job in east-end Toronto, Filipinos made up the largest ethnic group in my classes; teaching in Brampton, it was the Caribbean population that predominated at first, and then there was an influx of south-Asian immigrants. This is the story of Canada, a country that has welcomed large numbers of immigrants throughout its history, giving it the multicultural character for which it is known and admired around the world.

As a student and later as a teacher and counsellor, I saw a powerful phenomenon at work in the lives of immigrant kids around me and those I would later work with. They lived in two worlds at once. At home and in their ethnic communities, they lived according to the norms of their culture of origin. When they came to school, they were compelled to adopt the norms of the dominant culture — a mixture of Canadian and American materialism and secularism. There were at least four major stresses in their lives:

1. The stress of adapting to Canadian culture
2. The effect of the stress experienced by their parents as they tried to adapt to the new culture
3. The stress of balancing the expectations of parents and the expectations of the dominant culture
4. The stress of learning a new language

These stresses were present whether the child was born in Canada or was a recent arrival.

This phenomenon represents a huge mental health issue that goes almost completely unaddressed in our schools and in our communities generally. Schools with large immigrant populations are more likely to address some of these issues or at least be sensitive to them. But what I found in most schools was an almost complete unconsciousness of these stresses, almost a denial that they existed — both in those who were experiencing them and in those around them. Quick assimilation was the primary goal. Any talk about the problems involved would slow the process down. The stress this creates is huge, and leads to much suffering:

- Low self-esteem among immigrant children who never feel they "fit in"
- Intense pressure among immigrant children to succeed in school
- Conflict between parents and children over the expectations imposed by two cultures
- The child's alienation from parents and grandparents who don't understand — even who are sometimes literally unable to speak the same language

The solution to these stresses lies first in awareness that the problem exists and then in talking about the issues involved. There are no quick fixes. They are inevitably part of such a radical life change, but they could be managed better than they are. Many of the largest school boards in the greater Toronto area now have programs specifically aimed at new Canadians, helping them through the process of assimilation as well as honouring their own cultural and religious heritage. In smaller centers where there are fewer immigrants, this may not be the case.

Immigration trauma is not only an issue for recent arrivals who are going through the process of assimilation. It is also an issue for adult children of the immigrant experience who continue to be affected. For many of these kids, there were no supports in place at all. There were no ESL (English as a Second Language) classes in most schools until the past few decades. Before that, children were just required to "pick up the language." Some children suffered academically as a result of the language barrier. Others became overachievers, determined to disprove the appearance of incompetence created by poor language skills.

At my school on parent-teacher night it was common to see a young child, perhaps eight or nine years old, translating what the teacher was saying about him. Many adults who came to Canada as children still suffer from feelings of inadequacy, of constantly having to prove themselves and demonstrate that they fit in. Some suffer from lingering feelings of embarrassment or confusion about their own culture and customs. Some overcompensate with highly conventional behaviour, abandoning all vestiges of their culture of origin.

For boys, the immigrant experience has a particular angle. We have talked about the importance of fathers and elders in a boy's life — men who are competent and strong, who show the boy "how to be a man." There is a wound for the immigrant father and the immigrant son when this modelling function is disrupted by the context in which it happens. The father may have trouble speaking English, or speak with a noticeable accent, or he may continue to wear the style of dress of his country of origin. To the extent that it is a father's role to initiate his son into the norms of the larger society, there can be feelings of inadequacy on both sides.

These are deep issues that both generations must reflect upon. There is a tendency to take responsibility for things over which we have no control. The *situation* is the cause of the stress, not the individuals who are going through it. Inner narratives of shame and disappointment must be transformed into narratives of pride, courage, and remarkable accomplishment. This mindset is easier for the immigrant to adopt long after the hard times are over. It needs to be fostered early on as well.

10

When Mom and Dad Don't Live Together

The way children experience and process divorce depends on which stages of the marriage they were present for and at which stage the actual separation occurs — if it occurs at all. Some parents are separated or divorced without ever physically separating. Some homes are "broken homes" even though everyone still lives there. Similarly, even after a physical separation, the marriage can go on in the form of power struggles, angry episodes, and poor communication. For the child, the triangle of me-Mom-Dad never comes to an end. We will always be a family — just a different kind of family. Parents have a great deal of control over what this experience will be for the child.

Six stages can be identified in the marriage-to-divorce trajectory:

Stage 1: The Honeymoon Stage
We all know about the honeymoon period, a dream time when the partner is idealized and all conflicts and doubts can be painted over with emotions, hopes, and dreams. Anything is possible.

Stage 2: The Getting-to-Know-You Stage
This is the morning-after stage when we begin to learn who the other person really is apart from all of our projections and idealizations. There can be lots of little fights and disagreements over small issues during this period. The love bond keeps things together, but a pattern begins to be established for dealing with conflict: discussion, dialogue, and compromise — or defending entrenched positions.

Stage 3: The Smooth Stage

This is the intact marriage. The marriage has become functional, even efficient — in preparation for the next step, the business of setting up a home and family. This is the period when we work on external things, and the emotional dimension beneath is often neglected. This may be the period when children enter the picture.

Stage 4: The Stage of Unseen Cracks

As extremes of hot and cold weather will crack surfaces over time, so will the highs and lows of life create cracks in a relationship. These cracks appear along internal lines where the relationship was weakest or where the greatest external stresses are felt. Issues are ignored or glossed over. Differences don't get discussed. Conflict goes unresolved. The source of these cracks may be found in the present or they may have existed from the beginning or even long before the couple met. If there are going to be children, they are usually present by this stage, adding stress to the relationship. This is the stage during which communication, empathy, and compromise must be learned and practised or the relationship will continue to crack.

Stage 5: The Stage of Visible Cracks

During this stage both partners, as well as those around them, become conscious of a problem in the relationship as a whole. Apart from the specific things they argue about, there seems to be an underlying systems failure in their ability to deal with those problems. This is the stage at which displays of conflict may occur in front of the children. Many couples will go out of their way to shield the children from their fighting, but this is not really possible. Children might not hear the yelling, but they feel the emotional climate in the home, and they absorb the emotional stress felt by Mom and Dad. As physician and renowned speaker Gabor Maté has said, the quality of the relationship between Mom and Dad is the air children breathe. When that air becomes toxic, there is no protecting a child from it. Some children will spend their whole childhoods breathing this air. It will become their normal, and they will be at risk of unconsciously reproducing this environment.

Stage 6: The Decision Stage

When the stresses in a relationship become this great, decisions need to be made. If they are not made consciously, they will be made unconsciously. Doing nothing is a choice and has just as many consequences as any other choice. Possible decisions include:

a.   Separate physically. Mom and Dad take up separate living arrangements and the children are shared in some way. This option is almost always eventually formalized in a legal divorce.

b.   Separate emotionally. Mom and Dad continue to live together, and the family stays intact as a conventional-looking family unit. Mom and Dad exist in separate spheres and try to have as little to do with each other as possible. This usually means sleeping in separate rooms (one parent will sometimes share a room with a child for lack of other space). The level of conflict varies in these situations depending on how much the two partners choose or are forced to interact.

c.   Continue at stage 5 (visible cracks) indefinitely. Continue to yell and fight on a regular basis. This becomes the family's normal.

d.   Seek help. Make changes. Learn new ways of communicating and resolving conflict. Deal with core issues from childhood and mental health issues.

Options B or C are not conducive to emotional health. Parents who stay together "for the sake of the children" may be doing more harm than good and may be just taking the easier route. Whether they separate emotionally or descend into a constant state of fighting, the children are presented with a template for marriage that they will carry into their own adulthood. Options A and D offer the best prospects for children, provided they lead to a fuller, richer, healthier experience of life. When people leave any toxic situation, it should be a choice for growth and change, a decision to develop one's potential more fully. If the marriage situation inhibits our growth as a person, then we must make sure we grow when we leave it. Too many separated and divorced people never really leave the marriage. They become mired in anger, regret, resentment, sadness, shame, and guilt. This preoccupation with past decisions serves no purpose in the present. It drains everyone of energy for change and growth. If we are going to make a radical life change, we need to model a positive approach for our children. We are not victims. This is not a tragedy or a failure. It is a choice to go in a different direction, to reinvent ourselves — something that can happen again and again throughout life.

The Language We Use About Divorce

The language we use for separation and divorce has a big influence on how we think about them. We talk about fixing, repairing, or saving a marriage. We talk about marriage breakdown, a broken home, a marriage falling apart or coming to an end. No family comes to an end while even one of its members is still living. We can choose the kind of language we want to use about the new forms of family relationships we are seeing all around us. We have come up with terms like *blended family* to describe the coming together of partners with previous families. This is an attempt at re-labelling, however uninspiring it might be. Words like *step-mother*, *step-father*, etc. carry negative and archaic overtones. Whatever labels we choose, we need to change our thinking about separation and divorce from the language of loss, damage, and failure to language that implies change, process, evolution, and transformation.

Boys and Divorce

The way a boy reacts to divorce will depend on which of the stages he lived through. If he was there during stages 4 and 5, "the smooth stage" and "the stage of unseen cracks," he will have a nostalgic view of what was lost, but he will also have a reference point by which to judge the current state of the marriage and form a judgment about whether it is better or worse than it was before. If the child was only there for stage 5, "the period of visible cracks," he may be glad to be free of the toxic atmosphere. As with so many experiences in life, much depends on the child's temperament, or specifically their level of sensitivity and adaptability. Some kids are more deeply affected by what happens to them. Some kids are better than others at adapting to new situations. How we deal with a child going through the process of separation and divorce must take their temperament into account. Some kids will need more help; some will need less. A couple of general rules apply:

- Listen to the child when *he* is ready to talk.
- Don't try to talk the child out of their feelings. "It'll be fun having two different bedrooms."
- Don't pass judgment on the child's feelings. "It's silly to be worried."
- Affirm the child's feelings. "I hear you."
- Speak honestly about what is happening and what is going to happen.
- Don't go into more detail than the child's age requires.
- Do not use the child as a confidant.
- Never criticize or judge the other parent in front of the child.
- Use the language of growth, change, and opportunity.
- Avoid the language of failure, damage, and ending.

Boys and the Single Mother

A boy's relationship to his mother can become highly charged during adolescence. This is one of those stages of separation I talked about earlier. For boys, the relationship with the *single* mother may be even more charged. She may have been his main emotional support throughout childhood. He is strongly bonded to her. When adolescence comes, and he needs to break from his mother, he can feel very conflicted about this. He may overreact and push his mother away, forcefully trying to establish emotional autonomy. Conversely, he may cling to his mother beyond an appropriate stage out of a need for security, feelings of loyalty, or guilt about abandoning her. The emotional life of the mother can also colour this period. If she is emotionally needy herself, she may be unwilling to let the boy achieve his independence, or she may unconsciously encourage his dependence. This is a case where the emotional health of the adult becomes an important influence on the emotional health of the child. If the single mother takes care of her own emotional needs, she will be better able to navigate the process of separation with her son.

I have worked with many single mothers over the years whose sons almost seemed to turn on them in adolescence. Often, the degree of pushing Mom away was directly proportional to the degree of attachment to Mom in childhood. For many boys, breaking free of Mom's gravitational field can require an incredible amount of energy. The boy is desperately trying to establish a distinct male identity, and he may do this by rejecting all things feminine, including his mother. In adolescence, we sometimes see boys adopt a hyper-masculine persona in an effort to break from childhood. It helps if the mother understands this dynamic so that she does not take his rejection personally. The boy is going through a process of self-redefinition. What he needs at this point are positive male role models who can show him that becoming a man does not mean rejecting feminine traits and does not require abuse or rejection of his mother.

Boys and the Single Father

Our culture has a narrative of the heroic single mother, abandoned by her husband, working long hours to make enough money to raise her children. She is a strong woman who instills a noble moral code and work ethic in her children. There is no equivalent myth for men. The narrative of the single father is one of a pathetic man living by himself in an apartment who sees his kids periodically if at all. He is variously depicted as disgruntled, incompetent, or self-centered. He is disconnected from his kids, he's awkward in his dealings with them, and he gains their affection with gifts and "doing fun stuff."

Most commonly it is mothers who have exclusive or majority custody of children in separated or divorced families. We need to do all we can to maintain the legitimate and important role of the biological father. There is a tendency sometimes to fall back on the stereotype that the nurturing mother can do it all, that the bumbling, irresponsible, self-centered father is dispensable. This has become too common a stereotype, and it becomes a self-fulfilling prophecy. We need to expect more from men, and we need to be open to it when they are willing to give it. We need them to be involved in their children's lives. This becomes difficult when children become objects in a struggle for power and control between Mom and Dad.

Even though Mom and Dad are separated, boys still learn from their fathers what it means to be a man and a father. If he ever finds himself separated or divorced, he will follow the template set by his father. We are building the template for a new kind of family — including the separated and divorced one. The members are still bound together biologically and should continue to have a joint influence on the children — for good. We need a narrative of the responsible, nurturing, involved single father. This will only happen when it is lived out on a large scale.

The Deadbeat Dad

Fathers who are separated or divorced and don't visit their children or don't pay financial support are the most extreme version of the absent father. We even have a socially accepted label for them: *Deadbeat Dad*. It would be easy to enumerate all the reasons why it is wrong for men not to take responsibility and pay their fair share, and we can debate ways of enforcing compliance, but the deeper question remains: what are the causes of this behaviour? What is it about the way men are raised and socialized that makes them abandon their commitments and responsibilities? How do these men see their former wives? How do they see their children?

One of the reasons men don't pay is rooted in the perpetual problem of power and control. One of the ongoing conflicts in every male's life is the attempt to control or at least come to terms with feminine energy. We see this phenomenon in homophobia, and in hostility toward the mother during adolescence, and we see it again in the anger and frustration men feel toward their former lovers. The extreme version of this conflict is seen in outward violence toward women, which can happen within marriage or after a split. The common denominator in all of these scenarios is the feeling of impotence — a feeling men will do anything to avoid. To hand over one's money to the person one has lost control over can be felt by the man to be seen as an expression of weakness. On a rational level, the money is for the benefit of the kids. On an emotional level, it can still feel like a surrender of power and control. The whole separation and divorce process can feel emasculating and humiliating to the man. This feeling is often so strong that it overrides his feelings for his own children. This is not how men want to feel, but it is how many do feel.

Again, we are taken back to earliest childhood, to the way men process feelings of powerlessness. These feelings are deeply connected to how they perceive their own value. "If I am powerless, I am worthless." Men who experienced a lot of humiliation in childhood have a much harder time with feelings of powerlessness in adulthood. "I'm never going to let that happen again. I am a man now. I am not a child. I can control this situation in a way I could not then." This is the logical root of much male thinking when they display cruel or insensitive behaviour. They are re-enacting a former humiliation and seeking a different outcome.

What relevance does this topic have for raising emotionally healthy boys? We must understand the origin and logic behind the anger men feel. For many boys, their earliest experiences with power and control involve some form of humiliation, some form of being exposed. To the extent that these experiences are repeated, they become deeply embedded, and a male will grow up with the default mode of doing whatever he can to avoid loss of power. Men find it hard to move away from the *he-who-never-loses-control* definition of manhood. When the humiliation or loss of power and control happens at the hands of a woman, his definition of manhood can become *he-who-always-has-feminine-energy-under-control*. This definition of manhood also results from male socialization that does not allow the whole spectrum of feelings — including feelings such as sadness and nurturance — feelings that become labelled feminine in a man's mind. Men have to redefine masculinity as a strength in and of itself, not as something one gains by controlling or rejecting others. When men view masculinity as a rejection of all things feminine, they don't just try to control and reject the feminine energy of women; they try to control and reject feminine energy within themselves. They lose half themselves in the process, and one thing that gets rejected is their caring, nurturing self. They see it as a weakness, something that makes them vulnerable. This is the dynamic that allows a man to abandon his children emotionally and economically. As long as boys are raised with humiliation, and as long as they are taught to reject their vulnerable nurturing side, they will suffer, and those around them will suffer. A man who abandons his children is a man cut off from his own emotional life.

Part 3

The Games Boys Play

We can learn so much about boys by looking at the games they play. This is where their true selves find expression, where their deepest needs are met. Play is not an imposed activity; it is a chosen activity. This makes it a form a self-expression. Whether it's rough and tumble play, fantasy play, or video games, play provides a reliable window into our boys' hearts and minds.

One of the most powerful ways we can connect with our children is to play *with* them. This does not mean organizing and controlling the play. It means enjoying the play on an equal footing with the child. Play, at its best, is democratic. When we give ourselves over to play, we relinquish all roles and power structures. We become children ourselves, and our children see us in a new and positive light. Many fathers feel unprepared to interact with their children because their own fathers did not spend much time with them. I tell them all they have to do is lie down on the floor — the kids will take it from there. They know what to do! Many mothers fall into the responsible authority figure role. They feel as though they are always being "the heavy." The solution is the same: get down on the floor and play.

11

Play: The Natural Language of Children

Play is the natural language of children. It is how they first encounter the world and how they make sense of it. Children communicate with the world through play, and they can even communicate with us through their play if we know how to listen, and if we can recover this mode of expression ourselves. We were all children once, and good parenting means recalling what we once knew, or experiencing the world the way we did when we were children. This is how we develop empathy for our children. For infants and children, their whole body is engaged when they play. As we grow up, we are trained to narrow our focus to our hands and eyes. The relationship between the hands, eyes, and brain eventually becomes the most important in the child's life. Adults enthusiastically promote this triangular relationship because it fits so well with school. (It is also, incidentally, the sensory triangle for screen time.) Hands, eyes, and brain activate sight and touch only. We must also remember to honour whole-body play.

Play-Fighting

Rough play is natural. It is also fun. We see it among young animals. Why would we not expect it among young children? Boys in particular seem to gravitate naturally toward rough play perhaps because of the influence of testosterone. In the past twenty or thirty years we became suspicious of rough play in children and eventually condemned it outright. Some have analyzed this prohibition as the product of feminist analysis that was concerned that rough play would later lead to violent behaviour. In fact, the opposite may be true. Rough play is not a training ground for violence. It is a training ground for positive social interaction. Neuroscientists Sergio and Vivien Pellis have summarized these findings in an article entitled "Play-Fighting During Early Childhood and its Role in Preventing Later Chronic Aggression." Consider some of their conclusions:

- In times past, when it was not suppressed, estimates of the amount of freely chosen play to involve RTP (rough and tumble play) indicate that for children, especially males, is about ten percent.
- In monkeys and apes, the lack of opportunity to engage in RTP with peers leads to a reduced capacity for emotional self-regulation and impoverished social skills.
- Children that engage in more RTP tend to be better liked by peers, over consecutive years exhibit better social skills, and, overall, perform more effectively in the school setting with regard to academic performance.
- Play-impoverished children may misread social cues and so escalate to aggression.
- Play-impoverished children may have a smaller toolkit of options for convincing peers to cooperate, and so may resort to aggression to gain some operational advantage.

The authors have done detailed research on play-fighting in young rats, examining how it relates to brain anatomy and brain chemistry. Scientists know that the biological development of rats mirrors that of humans in many significant ways. This makes the following of Pellis and Pellis's observations important:

Once weaned, young rats spend about an hour per day engaged in RTP. Depriving young rats of the opportunity to play over the juvenile period (akin to between five and eleven years of age for children) leads to a wide range of deficits, the core of which involve an inability to attenuate their emotional reaction to novel or frightening situations, and this is associated with social deficits. These deficits are seen in the play-deprived rats' failings to coordinate their movements with those of a social partner — critical for successful sexual union — and in their misreading of social signals — critical to prevent social encounters from escalating into aggression. Crucial to emotional self-regulation and social skills is the ability of the prefrontal cortex (PFC) to exert executive control over the options available.

The authors make an important distinction between rough and tumble play that is fun and that which is hurtful.

For RTP to remain playful, it has to be reciprocal. That is, partners have to show the restraint necessary to prevent one of the participants always gaining and maintaining the advantage. Also, RTP can be unpredictable and ambiguous. That is, participants cannot predict when or if they will lose control of the situation, nor how they will regain it. So, if one partner transgresses by being more forceful than expected, a decision has to be made as to whether that partner is abusing the situation or has just been carried away by exuberance.

As it turns out, rat mothers have the same dilemma as human mothers! In their article "The Function of Play in the Development of the Social Brain" the same authors theorize that play-fighting prevents later aggression because it "is designed to ensure that juveniles frequently experience an unpredictable loss of control." They call this the training-for-the-unexpected hypothesis: animals with play experience are less affected by unpredictable events and are better able to regulate their emotional reactions. The authors conclude that "play trains animals to be resilient" and "experiencing the unexpected improves self-regulation."

Eleven-year-old Logan gets into fights about once a week. He longs for rough play, and did not get enough of it as a child. Could his aggressive behaviour be linked to his "play-impoverishment"? Those who work with sexual assault victims have suggested that sex education classes should include discussions about the meaning of *mutual consent*. If researchers are correct, positive rough play is the first training ground for learning about mutual consent. In positive, fun, rough play between friends, no means no. When we think about developing a child's self-esteem, we don't think about rolling around on the living floor with them. Children who engage in rough and tumble play with Mom or Dad grow up to be more confident and more resilient. In a safe setting, they learn about their own desires and those of others, and how to read, negotiate, and respect the boundaries between the two.

Making a Mess: Structured Play Versus Unstructured Play

The topic of rough play is problematic precisely because it is unpredictable. We have become very fearful of exposing our children to any activity that is not highly controlled. Most play has become *structured* play, organized sports being the clearest example, but even playdates are highly regulated. Activities are planned in advance and carried out according to schedule. Crafts are pre-planned with the pieces cut out in advance. All the child has to do is paste together his components to make his look like the adult-made exemplar. This is not creativity. Highly structured play does not exercise the full range of human imagination — it limits it. All children learn from this is how to follow instructions. What they need is unstructured play. This is where children enter the world of imagination and, yes, anything can happen! Unstructured play allows the child to express emotion, exercise will, resolve internal conflicts, build social skills, and bond with others. Unstructured play teaches self-regulation.

I have a ping-pong table in my office. When I play for the first time with a very young child, say seven or eight years old, we do not keep score. We simply hit the ball back and forth. Inevitably, for the first few weeks or months the child takes delight in whacking the ball as hard as possible. I laugh and play along. The child soon realizes without my saying anything that we are spending most of our time going after the ball on the floor — which isn't that much fun. The child eventually begins to self-regulate in order to increase the challenge and fun of the game. What starts out in chaos leads naturally to some kind of order. I find this phenomenon over and over again in unstructured play. It begins in freedom and evolves into self-discipline. The first time a younger child paints with me, the greatest attraction is mixing the colours all together and making the water for the brush turn different colours. Putting paint on the paper is secondary. Without my saying anything, the child eventually moves beyond the water and colour-mixing play to putting something on paper. What we must learn to accept is that the water-and-colour-play stage was just as important and meaningful as the painting-a-picture stage. The whacking-the-ping-pong-ball stage was just as important and meaningful as the keeping-score stage.

Fantasy Play

We have discussed the importance of whole-body play and unstructured play. The vital engine that drives both is fantasy play. What is going on in the mind of the child during play? This is one of the greatest mysteries in the universe and must be approached with awe and respect. The human organism seeks what it needs. All behaviour has its own inner logic. Nowhere is this more true than in the realm of fantasy. I have a castle, a doll house, and a bin full of action figures in my office. Children as old as fourteen and fifteen will get down on the floor and begin to play out particular scenarios from their imaginations. Free play happens when a child feels safe and relaxed. Their mind opens, and they are able to work out many of the tensions held within them. A lot of fantasy play involves conflict (fighting between action figures) because the child is working out his own internal conflicts. The more he gets this out in fantasy play, the less he will need to get out in real-world situations. Play allows a child to *express* emotion. The alternative is to *suppress* it. That's when he begins *acting out* in other ways.

Fantasy play depends completely on the imagination. In education we have become preoccupied with knowledge and skills. We pay little attention to the imagination in schools, and when we do, we make sure the children follow a safe, prescribed path. "Imagine that you are planning a birthday party; write a paragraph explaining what you would do to prepare." Parents have picked up on school's obsession with knowledge and skills, and their greatest fear is that their child will *fall behind*. In this kind of mindset, imagination becomes frivolous. The following quote is famous both for what it says and for who said it. Albert Einstein is our icon of logical, rational intelligence. He said, "Imagination is more important than knowledge. For knowledge is limited to all we now know and understand, while imagination embraces the entire world, and all there ever will be to know and understand." Why are the implications of this truth ignored? We should give at least as much importance to the imagination as we do to knowledge — especially in childhood.

12

The Real Reason Boys Don't Take Ballet

Tyler was accepted into the vocal music program at a competitive arts school. It was a great accomplishment for this relatively shy boy, but he would not tell anyone in his grade eight class. When one of his friends did find out, Tyler got the response he feared most — he was called *gay*. In this episode we see several aspects of the tragedy of male experience. As girls grow up, they are permitted, indeed encouraged, to pursue a wide range of activities, even those considered traditionally male. Boys have not had the same kind of liberation. As they grow up, their options become narrower. They avoid any activities or behaviours that are seen as feminine. These are *gay*. Whole areas of human life become out of bounds or require great personal courage to enter, most notably the arts and human services. Boys do not generally consider becoming dancers, singers, artists, nurses, or elementary school teachers. Why is this the case?

The answer may sound contradictory, but let's see where the logic leads. It happens because we deny boy energy from a very young age. We encourage a kind of cuddly, non-violent, "use-your-words" identity. There are to be no guns, no stories with guns, no killing, and no hurting. It is a neutered world where feelings of aggression, competition, anger, frustration, and hostility are all denied. We seem to feel that if we simply deny these dark or negative feelings, they will go away. They do not go away, and they are not even dark or negative. They simply are. But when they are denied, they persist and grow stronger and come out in deformed ways in adolescence. The soft pastel world of childhood becomes the springboard into its antithesis — the shallow, rude, crude, violent, blood-and-guts, no-regard-for-anyone-else world of video games and adolescent male popular culture. In short, a feminized boyhood leads to a hyper-masculine adolescence, in some cases even a misogynistic adolescence. One extreme leads to another extreme. We create the conditions in childhood for losing our boys in adolescence. When a boy reaches his teen years, he feels the need to break from the primary mother bond. This is healthy and natural. He has to define himself as distinct from his mother and women generally, and so he turns to all those things denied him in boyhood: aggressive, assertive energy — boy energy. All things feminine become *gay* when seen in a male, and he is left with a distorted concept of what it means to be a man — tough, silent, unfeeling. He is limited to half the repertoire of human emotion and human behaviour. The last thing in the world he would ever consider would be taking ballet!

The situation becomes especially problematic if the boy has been raised solely by his mother. This is too commonly the case after separation or divorce, but in some homes, even though Dad is physically present, his male energy is not felt. He joins in the pastel parenting, and the boy has no model of positive male energy in childhood. Ideally, Dad will be more likely to accept, celebrate, and even share in boy energy. The problem is not the instilling of feminine characteristics in boys. Boys need mothers, and they need what mothers teach. These feminine characteristics are, in fact, not exclusively feminine. They exist in all of us. The problem is the polarization of gender characteristics, like the examples in this table.

Boy Energy	Girl Energy
Rough play	Quiet play
Spontaneous movement	Controlled movement
Squirming	Sitting still
"Outside voice"	"Inside voice"
Assertiveness	Well-behaved

Aggression	Holding back
Competition	Co-operation
Going first	Others first
Self-assertion	Waiting one's turn
Self-reliance	Reliance on others
Concrete thinking	Abstract thinking
Communicating through action	"Use your words"

If a broader range of behaviour was permitted in childhood among both sexes, we wouldn't have the dark side of this polarization in adolescence. "When I pull that doll's arms and legs off, it's just a doll. It's an object. You think that if I pull dolls' arms and legs off now, I will be mean to women later on, but the truth is if you don't let me objectify this doll, I might objectify people later on. Let me get it out now rather than later. Let me get a lot of things out now, when they are real and powerful to me. Don't be afraid of my kid feelings acted out in kid fantasy. I am learning the difference between the inner world and the outer world, between play and real life, but for now my play is real life; don't take that from me." So many of the negative things we see in adolescent-boy-world are there because they were denied in kid-world. Too many of them were denied because they involved one key ingredient — boy energy.

Should Boys Be Allowed to Play with Guns?

The following story illustrates how much North American society has changed in the past forty years. When I was about ten years old, the Knights of Columbus (a Catholic men's organization) had a Christmas party for members' families. The climax of the party was a visit by Santa Claus who handed out presents to each child. All the boys within a certain age range, including me, were given guns. To me my toy gun was the most beautiful object in the world. It was a plastic machine gun that looked very realistic and made a great noise. I loved that gun! My best friend, George, was at the same party and got the same gun. For the next few years a lot of our play revolved around those guns. The only negative thing I remember about that period were the arguments that ensued when George or I would refuse to admit we had been killed. The rule was the victim had to lie down and count to a certain number before he could resume play. George and I did not often fight against each other. We preferred to fight together against a common imaginary foe. That was more fun. One summer, one of our neighbours was building an extension onto their house, which involved the presence of a large excavating truck. For about a week, we stalked that monster, that dinosaur, that enemy tank. Another time, one of the neighbours cut down a huge willow tree and we spent several days in the jungle crawling through the branches of that tree looking for the enemy.

The fantasies around those guns were of courage, risk-taking, and achieving challenging goals. Boys are fascinated by fighting and war because they see it as an arena in which to prove themselves, an arena in which they might find out what they are made of. This process is essential to boys because they are not sure what we are made of. They sense their unique masculine nature, but they are not sure what it is — and so they try to test it out. They try to find it through experience. The nature boys are discovering in themselves through fighting and war play is not an essentially violent or destructive nature; it is an assertive, competitive, goal-oriented nature. It is also a protective nature. It is a nature that finds joy in movement! Coming to terms with this energy is an essential stage in the psychic development of every boy. Denial of this energy or the attempt to sublimate it into other forms is not the answer.

I am not suggesting that guns are an essential toy for boys or that war play needs to be part of every boy's play experience. I am citing guns and war play as the most blatant and visible example of boy energy manifesting itself. It can take many other forms, which are also discouraged and viewed with suspicion. Guns and war play are the easiest target for the denial of boy energy. There are lots of political, sociological, and psychological reasons why these toys and games should not be encouraged, but when this energy erupts spontaneously in gun play or war play (or even with a stick), it need not be seen as pathological. The great irony is that the generation of boys who grew up not being allowed to play with guns or even include guns in their stories at school now spend countless hours in front of glowing screens in dark basements shooting and shooting and shooting. They are still working out their relationship to their own male energy — something that should have happened through the developmental stages of childhood and adolescence but was denied — and they are stuck in a kind of loop, trying to figure it out, trying to understand what it means to be a man.

If a boy is permitted to work through this stage, to feel his energy, to exert his power, he will move on to further horizons. Real wars are waged by under-developed men, men still stuck in a child-like need to feel their personal power by exerting it over others. When we look at the biographies of violent dictators, we always find arrested development. These men are stuck in boyish war play; they need to prove themselves; they need to define themselves by dominating others. The cycle of violence continues among men who have never moved beyond the boy stage.

13

Screen Time

One of the biggest challenges facing parents today is the impact of technology on their children. Anyone growing up before about 1980 had one screen to deal with — the TV. Kids today are growing up with at least four screens that dominate their lives: television, computers (which includes tablets), video games, and cell phones. Screen time in itself is not the problem. There is nothing inherently damaging about being at a screen. It is a question of the quantity and quality of screen time that needs to be examined. I talked earlier about the need for a balanced sensory diet. Screen time is a feast for one sense — the visual. None of the other senses are getting a workout and certainly the body is not getting any kind of workout. Children need a varied sensory diet as they are growing up. The principle of brain development is *use it or lose it*. The parts of the brain we use will develop; the parts we do not use will atrophy. I talk to kids about neural pathways and show them a picture of a barely-discernable walking path through the woods. Then I show them a picture of a multi-lane super highway with all kinds of underpasses and overpasses. I explain to them that both of these pictures represent neural pathways. The faint path through the forest is, for many boys, the logical, linear, linguistic pathway. The super highway is a picture of their visual-spatial functioning. Many boys have developed their visual-spatial ability to an astonishing degree and neglected their verbal-linguistic functioning. The reason this is such an important problem is that school rewards logical, linear, verbal functioning much more than visual-spatial functioning. One of the reasons boys are falling behind in school is because of the inordinate amount of time they are spending at screens outside of school. Their brains are not being exercised for what school demands.

Television is a passive medium. We just sit there and let it wash over us. Modern screens have the advantage of being interactive. They require something of the viewer, some kind of response and *activity*. The important question becomes what kind of activity is one doing on the screen? Here the options are endless, but for most kids they seem to fall into two main categories: gaming and social media. Statistically, boys gravitate toward gaming and girls toward social media. We can learn a lot about our boys by studying what they love.

Ten Things Video Games Can Teach Us About Parenting Boys

1. The Need to Move in Space
The male brain has evolved over millions of years to be good at two things — seeing and moving through space. Video games are a feast of what the male brain loves most. The boy on his video game is a hunter-gatherer moving through terrain, looking with great intensity for the kill. Video games are here to stay and will become more sophisticated in the future.

Implications for Parenting
We need to get our boys out moving through real space. Team sports provide the same kind of pleasure video games do. Sports have many benefits that gaming does not have, most notably physical exercise and social interaction. The disadvantages of sports include having to wait one's turn, not being played, or possibly having to put up with a negative coach or peer group. Individual activities such as hiking, camping, boating, or skiing (downhill or cross country) provide the same spatial stimulation as team sports do.

2. Addictive Behaviour
Video games can be addictive for the male brain because they increase production of the neurotransmitter dopamine which plays a vital role in the brain's reward and pleasure centers. The pleasure is further intensified

by the randomness of this gratification, its sudden onset and quick reso-lution. Something or someone pops up, and one has to deal with it spon-taneously. The level of difficulty must be just within the player's grasp, so there is enough reward to keep him playing. Video games do this perfectly.

Implications for Parenting
Find pleasure-inducing activities that have more productive outcomes and more positive side-effects. Psychiatrist William Glasser wrote a book called *Positive Addiction,* in which he suggested that people could harness their addictive tendencies for good. He was one of the first to talk about the *runner's high* — the concept that exercise can release dopamine and endorphins. Pay attention to the other interests shown by boys and encourage those interests. One of the reasons boys spend so many hours online is that there really is "nothing else to do."

3. The Need for Power and Control

Video games are so attractive to males because of the sense of personal power they give to the user. The thing we hold in our hand is called a *controller* and that is exactly where a large part of the pleasure lies. This raises the all-important question of kids and personal power. Too many kids feel powerless in their lives. As I discussed earlier, they are micro-managed by parents and school. Everyone around them has an agenda, expectations — a long list of "shoulds." This has a debilitating effect on kids, particular-ly by early adolescence when their own need for autonomy is growing by leaps and bounds. "When I'm on the screen, I am in charge of my own life. When I come off the screen, other people are in charge." That is how many kids feel. We drive our kids onto the screen by not allowing them greater autonomy in their wider lives. For kids in their twenties, the situation is much more difficult. The unemployed twenty-three-year-old living in his parents' basement who spends the night gaming is living out a fantasy of male power that he cannot find in the real world. Unlike the child and adolescent who escape into video games to avoid Mom, Dad, and school, the twenty-something is escaping from an economic system that has no place for him. With youth unemployment at record levels in the Western world, it is no wonder so many young men have turned to gaming.

Implications for Parenting

At the family level, we need to give our children a greater sense of autonomy and self-directedness from a young age. We discussed this at length in the sections on self-monitoring and self-regulation. At the larger societal level, we need to create an economic climate and an entrepreneurial spirit in our youth that will motivate them to create jobs rather than just looking for them. They will not just do one kind of training for one kind of job. Statistics show that most people in the workforce today will have many jobs, will have to retrain several times and will have to be flexible and innovative in their approach to work. The worker of the future needs to think of himself as the one in control of his own career. The power lies with him. He is not a victim of economics. He is not passively dependent on others to hire him. We must instill these mindsets at an early age.

4. The Need for Concrete Goals

Boys love goals. The goal of every video game is clear and attainable with some reasonable degree of effort. When the goal is achieved, there is a feeling of satisfaction, and one immediately moves on to the next reward experience. There are clear levels and a clear system of moving up through those levels. Perseverance and overcoming obstacles is valued and rewarded in video games.

Implications for Parenting (and Teaching)

When our child expresses an interest in something, he will usually have a goal in mind. He wants to build a tree fort, catch a fish, or win a contest or trophy. As I mentioned earlier, we must do all we can to facilitate the child's interests beyond video games, and just as importantly, encourage him to achieve his goals, whether we think they have value or not. Many activities, such as swimming and martial arts, have levels through which one progresses. Boys like this clarity and sense of a concrete, measurable process. If this is the case with our sons, then we should seek those activities out. The other important thing about goals is the perseverance factor — committing to the project and sticking with it even through times of discouragement. Boys do this all the time in video games. They can learn it in real-world activities even better.

School could learn something from video games too. While it is true that school has grade levels and marks as rewards, these often seem very abstract or subjective to students. Teachers could apply the principle of creating concrete, measurable goals. "What is it exactly you want me to do?" Academic evaluation will always include a subjective element, and some courses have it far more than others. This can drive boys crazy. "Why did I get that mark?" Boys like multiple choice or one-word-answer questions because success or failure is clear. Boys have been shown to do better than girls on multiple choice tests like the SATs in the United States. Statistically, boys prefer math partly because their brains are better wired for it but also because of the right-or-wrong-answer aspect of math. Boys fume at the marks given to the process — "show your work." In their minds, the answer is enough. They either got it or they didn't. As an English teacher handing back essays, I would often get the question, "What did I get wrong?" If a boy gets a 75 percent with the comment "poor structure," he will say he lost twenty-five marks for structure.

There is a downside to the concrete approach, however. Evaluation rubrics can become so prescriptive that they actually constrain learning. For those activities that are more nuanced, like writing, we need to do a better job at explaining the subtleties that make up good writing. One of the traps we have fallen into in the arts and humanities is turning abstract, nuanced activities like writing into concrete activities. Some "essay planners" spell out what every sentence in the essay should "do." When students follow this strict outline, they are no longer writing an expository essay. They are stringing together a long series of answers to questions or directives from the essay planner. Their own thought processes are not developed. They are only learning to say what the teacher wants. These essays are also easier for teachers to mark. They either jumped through the hoops listed or they didn't. Truly creative and original writing is much harder to evaluate, and there is much less of it going on in our schools today. Boys need to be given concrete tasks with concrete goals, but they must also be challenged to develop their abstract thinking and the attainment of abstract goals.

5. The Need for Territory

A by-product of the male brain's love of movement and space is his awareness of territory. Football is the best sport to illustrate this phenomenon,
but it exists in most sports and in most video games. Invading territory,
defending territory, gaining territory, and controlling territory — these
are all pleasure-inducing experiences for the male brain. But, ultimately,
there is pleasure in simply moving through territory and taking in the
way it looks. When new versions of video games come out, one of the
things boys are most interested in are the new landscapes.

Implications for Parenting

The territory in video games is not real. The whole environment is artificial. We need to immerse our children in nature as much as virtual reality. Kids can move through complex game landscapes, but they
cannot point out north or south where they live. I know teenagers who
cannot explain how to get to the next town or where cities are in re-
lation to each other. They are not even able to name the streets that
branch off from their own. As kids stay inside more, they have literally
lost contact with the physical spatial environment in which they live.
It is important that our children learn to know where they are in the
world and what lies at the periphery of their world. It is important to
explore and expand this periphery. We need to tell them "the world is
your playground — go out and enjoy it, get to know it, and yes, even
take care of it." I fear for the future of the environment for the simple
fact that so few kids even know where it is. They have travelled miles in
their virtual worlds of pixilated landscapes but have never explored the
real woods at the edge of their subdivision.

6. The Need for Rewards

There are two kinds of rewards — intrinsic and extrinsic. A classic
statement of the intrinsic reward is the pleasure of a job well done.
Volunteer work, when done out of a real sense of charity, has its own
intrinsic rewards. Whatever hobbies we do, we do for the enjoyment
they bring. That is the main payoff. Parenting is intrinsically rewarding. Extrinsic rewards are outside the activity itself. The pay we get
for working would be the most obvious example. Gaming involves

both reward systems. It is pleasurable in itself and there is also a very concrete system of rewards in the form of points and levels and other things earned. On the screen of most video games, there is almost always a box somewhere (sometimes several) giving a constant stream of reward feedback in the form of numbers or symbols. The gamer always knows where he stands. Gaming is like the perfect job — getting paid for what one loves to do constantly as one is doing it.

Implications for Parenting

Gaming could be seen as a template for life. People who really love their job refer to it as fun. We can help our children look for something they love to do that pays, exploring questions with them like, "What do you find intrinsically rewarding that other people would be willing to reward you extrinsically for? What 'game' could you play in the real world that would provide you with an income?" Many young boys dream of making their living as video game testers. While this may be unrealistic, there are many skills associated with video games that could point to career possibilities: computer programing, graphic design, and machine operator (to name only a few).

In terms of extrinsic rewards, there are some boys who are motivated by the payoff. Many parents use a reward system for chores, homework, or good behaviour. This can be an effective tool as long as it is done in moderation, and as long as there are still areas of boy's life where he does things just because they are reasonable expectations.

7. The Need to Deal with Emotions

Some boys like video games because they are an escape from the stress of life, from feelings of disappointment, powerlessness, and anger, and from fear of failure. There are many logical reasons to escape into cyberspace when real life is uncomfortable. The world of gaming is simple, clean, and predictable. The boy always knows where he stands. The rules are clear, and everyone follows them. The consequences for compliance and non-compliance are completely consistent and concrete. Video games are programmed. Life is not. The emotional world of video games is very simple compared to the complex emotional world of real life. Many males do not have the emotional vocabulary or the practice of dealing with their emotions. Their emotions lie in *terra incognita* (unknown land) — at the edges of the map. "Here be dragons" old maps used to have printed at their edges. That is how so many males feel about their feelings — scared — as though their feelings are menacing dragons to be avoided at all costs. When I am working with a male who is suffering from some problem that has become too big to ignore, one of the first barriers we have to pass through is talking about feelings. I use the metaphor of the dragon, and I tell them that "in order to slay a dragon first you have to face it. You can't deal with something you refuse to admit is even there." It is ironic that video games celebrate male courage and bold action toward the enemy, but that those playing are often deathly afraid of the real adversaries in their own lives. Killing virtual enemies becomes a metaphor and a substitute for all the things the person is not facing or dealing with.

Implications for Parenting

We need to train our boys to have an emotional vocabulary from an early age. This must continue into adolescence when their emotional temperature rises even higher. The emotional roller coaster of the teenage years requires guidance and support. Boys need role models, and they need people who will listen. In childhood the mother is the main teacher of emotional intelligence. Dad needs to be there too. When boys reach adolescence, they will often reject or supress in themselves all those things they associate with femininity. Talking about feelings is one of these. They put on what William Pollack, noted researcher on men's issues, calls the emotional straightjacket. Unfortunately, many video games promote the hyper-masculine man who shows no feelings. Real-life men need to provide an antidote to this unbalanced picture of manhood.

If a boy is exposed to emotionally intelligent men in his childhood, he is more likely to allow his emotional life the space it needs when he reaches adolescence.

8. The Need for Guidance with Gender Relations and Gender Roles

It is interesting to note that interactions with the opposite sex are almost non-existent in most video games. It is a male world of males relating to other males in male ways. This is a good thing and a bad thing.

It is a good thing because males benefit from time spent with other males in the same way that females benefit from time spent with other females. There is something bonding and reinforcing about being with other people of one's own gender. Boys develop their male identities through interaction with other males. Certain characteristics are reinforced and others not. Again, this can be a good thing or a bad thing depending on the peer group we are exposed to. For millions of years males as hunter-gatherers spent most of their time with other males, and females in their nurturing role spent most of their time with other females. Only in recent history have men and women spent so much time together. Both genders have a natural need to be amongst themselves and in gaming this need is met.

The downside of the male-only video-game world is the lack of practice it provides in dealing with females. While it is true that males learn who they are with other males, it is just as true that they learn who they are from interactions with females. Boys need to be around females in order to learn how they behave, relate, and think. Not that these ways are totally different from the way males behave, relate, and think. In fact, a male can find out just as much about himself from a woman as he can from a man — perhaps more. What we stereotype as feminine qualities are found in all men, and when males interact with women, these qualities are affirmed and strengthened. This is particularly important in adolescence. In childhood, gender roles have not become entrenched so we give both boys and girls a broad range of "acceptable" behaviour. By adolescence the gender role stereotypes come crashing down and boys and girls can become locked into very restrictive roles. Video games run the danger of reinforcing these gender stereotypes. The gaming world has very strict gender roles. The male is aggressive, emotionless, destructive, and competitive at all costs. Women are either cast in the typical passive sex-object role or they themselves are aggressive, emotionless fighters. It is interesting that some boys will choose a female avatar when playing video games. She is like a female man. I see in this some attempt on the part of the boy to retain the feminine. That is the problem of adolescence: the jettisoning of the feminine. The little boy who was happy to sing and dance and draw, the boy who cried easily and spoke freely about all his emotions, shuts that all down when he reaches adolescence. It is one of the greatest tragedies in the male story: the abandonment of those things that get labelled feminine.

Implications for Parenting

Boys need male-only time, but they also need to be around girls. Young boys will often have female friends just as easily as male friends. These relationships should be encouraged and be on equal footing with those with other boys. As boys get older, they need social experiences with girls. These are getting harder to find in our culture. Hanging out (unstructured social time) is an important experience for adolescents. How can we create opportunities for hanging out with both male and female neighbours, friends, and cousins? Even at younger ages, birthday parties and playdates do not have to be boy-only events.

Boys also need to be exposed to all those activities that are increasingly being labelled as feminine — especially the arts. Boys need to be exposed to art, theatre, dance, and music. This exposure does not have to be through stuffy experiences of long Shakespearean plays, or ballets, or symphonies. There are lots of contemporary avant-garde productions that are edgy, provocative, and "cool." There are lots of art galleries with interactive kid spaces. For younger boys, encourage the singing they do in the car, the dancing they do around the house, the way they cry at movies and draw Valentine cards for their mothers. Dad must encourage these activities as well, especially as the boy gets older. By ten or eleven, the boy will start to shut down if these emotional outlets are not encouraged by both parents.

9. The Need for a Social Life

Statistically, boys are predominantly drawn to video games whereas girls tend to gravitate more toward social media. One of the reasons boys play video games is the same reason girls go to social networking sites — the need for connection. All people seek human connection, and while boys are sometimes depicted as not needing it as much, they need it as much as anyone. They are also socialized out of this need — taught to ignore it or reject it altogether. With the advent of online gaming, the variety of possibilities for connection has increased. In the beginning, video games were played alone or by two people sitting together. This was a good arrangement because the boys were in each other's physical presence. One had to go over to someone else's house to play. Since video games went online, the experience has changed drastically. Physical proximity is now gone, and the physical presence of the other players has been replaced by constructed avatars. There is still tone of voice, however, which is a good thing, although the incidence of foul and abusive language increased when boys became disembodied and only virtually present. Boys meet up with school friends online, but they also meet other people. Some boys refer to their "Xbox friends" or their "gaming friends." Online gaming has produced a greater variety of social interactions, but those interactions have become more superficial and artificial. When boys are playing online they are not getting to know each other better, and they are not revealing much of importance about themselves. Adolescent boys can find social interaction difficult at the best of times. Gaming has increased the number of *contacts* boys have, but it has also increased their sense of social disconnection simply because they have far fewer opportunities to practise the full range of social behaviour — interpreting tone of voice, reading facial expression, and other nuances of face-to-face contact. This is true for boys' interaction with other boys and even truer for boys' interaction with girls from whom they tend to become even more disconnected during adolescence because of gaming.

Implications for Parenting

School and the classroom have become the last public arenas in which social skills can be practised. Class discussions and group work are more important as kids have less exposure to organic, unpredictable social interaction. In addition to school, it is vitally important for parents to create opportunities for boys to practise social skills by creating opportunities for kids to gather among themselves or with adults. Encouraging your child to have kids over to the house or to go to other kids houses becomes important for their development of relationships at a deeper level. Family activities take on greater importance for kids who are spending so much time on screens. It comes back to the issue of balance. Screen time is fine, but it must be balanced with face-to-face time and real-world time.

10. The Need for Play

In our fast-paced, school-based culture, children do not get enough time for play. They are quickly launched into programs, lessons, and activities of all sorts. Most of these involve some kind of monitoring adult. Play is the default mode for children. They are taken from this world too soon. Video games provide a return to this world for adolescents. Even though the environment is highly structured, the child perceives it as a place of spontaneity, power, and control. "It's fun because I can do whatever I want," they tell me. This is one of the attractions of the Grand Theft Auto series, for example. There are story lines and missions that one could play, but most kids just drive around crashing into people and objects. It is a world where the laws of appropriate behaviour do not apply. It is a playground for the adolescent. Interestingly, many men play these kinds of games as well. The same impulse is at work — a desire for escape into the world of play. The famous educator A.S. Neill once said that no child ever gets enough play, and that this unmet need continues into adulthood where we see many adults who are still stuck in the play stage. Neill believed that only when the play stage was fully *played out* would an adult be able to move on and fully devote himself to the demands of adulthood.

Implications for Parenting

Make sure children have as much opportunity for unstructured free play as possible before they discover video games, and hold off on video games as long as possible. We don't want to turn video games into a forbidden fruit, nor do we want to make it the default mode of play for the young child. For reasons mentioned earlier, it is "virtual play" or to put it more bluntly, it is artificial play. The world is not real, the movement is not real, and the fantasy scenario is not one's own.

The Benefits of Playing Video Games

A major study entitled "The Benefits of Playing Video Games" by Isabela Granic, Adam Lobel, and Rutger Engels was published in *American Psychologist*, a journal of the American Psychological Association, in January 2014. The article summarizes the findings of a number of research projects, all looking into the benefits of playing video games. The results are important to the current debate on whether video games are good or bad for kids. The article breaks the benefits down into four domains: cognitive, motivational, emotional, and social.

Cognitive Benefits of Gaming

According to the study, gaming leads to "faster and more accurate attention allocation." This means knowing what to pay attention to and making these decisions quickly. This has to do with filtering out extraneous visual information and getting to the most important information fast. Kids who play video games were also shown to have "higher spatial resolution in visual processing." This means seeing more accurately and knowing exactly what one is looking at in order to make the best decisions about it. Gaming also leads to "enhanced mental rotation abilities." This refers to the ability to imagine objects from other points of view, to see a situation from all sides. Finally, the authors state that gaming is an excellent means for developing problem-solving skills. Video games involve a constantly changing series of problems to be solved. Decisions need to be based on a quick and accurate assessment of the visual information and confidence to act to solve the problem quickly.

Motivational Benefits of Gaming

The study showed that gaming teaches that persistence in the face of failure reaps valued rewards. This is an important lesson for life. We have all seen incredible persistence in kids playing video games. They will not come off the game until they have achieved their goal. If this same attitude could be applied in other situations, the possibilities would be endless. The answer lies in the reward system. The rewards in video games are simply points and levels. In school the rewards are similar — marks and grades. The difference is that the goals and reward structure of video games are much simpler, clearer and, in the mind of the gamer, fairer. In many ways the game of school feels rigged. Some players have advantages over others and the game masters keep changing the rules. One never really knows where one stands. There is currently much talk in education about the gamification of school. School has always been a game. Perhaps it will become a better one when we admit that this is what it is and design it better as a game. The authors also state that video games are very good at finding the "'zone of proximal development.' This motivational 'sweet spot' balances optimal levels of challenge and frustration with sufficient experiences of success and accomplishment." Here is another principle school could learn from. For many kids, the work at school oscillates between too easy and too hard. Because the curriculum is fixed, it does not always match the strengths and weaknesses of the student. Students may not be challenged in their area of strength, or their area of weakness might receive no remediation. Games do not have a fixed curriculum. The game is interactive; it responds to the ability of the player. Schools are not interactive in this way.

Emotional Benefits of Gaming

The authors also found that gaming helps kids "manage moods." Managing one's mood can refer to going from a state of arousal (brought on by feelings of stress, anger, frustration, fear) to a relaxed state, or it can also mean going in the opposite direction from a state of boredom, apathy, or depression to an aroused state. Some people manage their moods with exercise, music, shopping, or simply watching TV. Some use coffee, alcohol, or drugs. We can see that some of these mood-managing techniques are healthier than others. To determine if something is healthy or not, we look at side-effects and frequency of use. Negative side-effects increase with frequency of use. The most positive activity can become detrimental if it is done to excess. So the question of whether or not gaming is a valid way of managing one's mood becomes a question of how much gaming is too much. When does the harm outweigh the benefits? For other substances and behaviours, we ask questions like:

- Is it affecting your physical health?
- Is it affecting your emotional health?
- Is it affecting your relationships?
- Is it affecting your ability to function productively?

When the answers to too many of these questions is yes, then we conclude there is a problem. This analysis is valid for any substance or behaviour we use to manage moods, including gaming.

The researchers conclude that gaming can "enhance emotional states." This could be a good thing or a bad thing. A video game might make a happy kid happier, an angry kid angrier, or an isolated kid more isolated. In the last two cases, we need to focus on the child, not the video game. Why is the child angry? Why does the child feel isolated? Overuse of video games might be a symptom of other problems, not the problem itself. The authors choose to focus on the positive. "Gaming may be among the most efficient and effective means by which children and youth generate positive feelings."

Social Benefits of Gaming

The study found that over 70 percent of gamers play with a friend. This does not mean going over to each other's house and physically playing together. It means playing online. Gaming is the new *going outside to play*. It's just a different kind of outside. The authors state, "In these virtual social communities, decisions need to be made on the fly about whom to trust, whom to reject, and how to most effectively lead a group. Given these immersive social contexts, we propose that gamers are rapidly learning social skills and prosocial behaviour that might generalize to their peer and family relations outside the gaming environment." They go on to say that "Players seem to acquire important prosocial skills when they play games that are specifically designed to reward effective cooperation, support, and helping behaviour," and the research suggests that this is equally true for violent and non-violent games!

I have known and spoken intimately with countless gamers over the years, and I have consistently found them to be kind, civilized, articulate, and socially adept. But they may not show these qualities at school or among their peers because they find both to be very shallow and artificial compared with the gaming world. They see school world as something to be tolerated until they can get back to the more legitimate and rewarding world of gaming. Many video games involve working within a clan or group. Boys can become very committed to these groups and derive self-esteem from their contribution. They also get to know things about each other that one would not expect. Liam, a seventeen-year-old with a severe stutter, connected online with another boy who had the same issue, and they soon extended their relationship outside the gaming world.

Coming Off Video Games

To achieve greater compliance when coming off video games, parents must understand two factors at work. The first is the phenomenon of hyper-focusing; the second is the difficult dynamic of transitioning. The female brain is good at focusing on a number of things simultaneously and moving between these centres of focus. The male brain, on the other hand, prefers to focus on one thing at a time, and when that activity is particularly engaging, he can hyper-focus with great intensity for a long period of time. If we go back to the hunter-gatherer brain, the ability to focus intensely on something for a long period of time, as in tracking an animal for example, brought natural rewards for survival. This ability persists, and males are capable of intense focus for quite a long time. (Incidentally, this is also true of kids with ADHD. It's not that they can't pay attention. In fact, kids with ADHD are capable of intense focus. They have trouble *regulating* their attention, which means they cannot pay attention to things they find boring or which seem to have no purpose. This ability to hyper-focus was an advantage in hunting and gathering, but it's not usually an advantage in the classroom.)

An appreciation of the phenomenon of hyper-focusing leads to the issue of transitioning. A boy who is hyper-focusing on anything, like a video game, will require time and effort to disengage from that activity. He may also require some coaxing and coaching and other external strategies. Here are a few:

- Watch the game for transitional moments when it can be paused. When we ask a boy to come off in the middle of an intense battle, he will not be very compliant. Ask, "Where can you pause it?" When he says, "Just let me finish this part," that might be a reasonable solution.
- Give warnings. "We're leaving in half an hour … we're leaving in fifteen minutes …"

- Allow for delays. If we know we have to be out the door by seven o'clock, make it very clear that we have to be out the door by six-thirty.
- Mental rehearsal. "The last time we were over at your cousin's, there was a big fight when it was time to leave and I asked you to come off the video game. Tonight I'm going to come downstairs at eight o'clock and say, 'We're leaving in half an hour.' Then I'm going to come downstairs fifteen minutes later and say, 'We're leaving in fifteen minutes.' Then I'm going to come down at eight-thirty and say it's time to go, and you are going to come off the video game, come upstairs, say goodbye to everyone, and we're going to head out the door and get in the car." This is a type of neuro-linguistic programming. It is not said in any shaming or threatening way. It is simply an objective, external description of what is going to happen. It works!

What Should the Limits Be?

According to the The American Academy of Pediatrics, "Children and teens should engage with entertainment media for no more than one or two hours per day, and that should be high-quality content." In my work with parents, I recommend the following limits as maximums:

- One hour at a sitting
- Two one-hour sittings for every five hours of free time

The child gets home at four o'clock; he goes to bed at nine o'clock. That's five hours. A valid routine would be one hour of screen time before dinner and one hour after dinner. This would be a *maximum* arrangement for a child or teenager. Less than that, particularly for younger children, is great.

A fundamental question when it comes to regulating screen time is what are the alternative activities available? Kids play video games because they are so seductive. It is hard to get off something so pleasurable. They also play video games because nothing else is so readily available.

Alternatives to Screen Time

We need to *normalize* other activities such as outside play, reading, talking together, and having meals together. When we make something a routine, it becomes *taken for granted*. Going outside should simply be part of the daily routine. This is just something we always do. If we do this when kids are very young, it becomes imprinted. Dr. Maxwell Maltz famously said it takes twenty-one days to form a habit. It takes much less than twenty-one days to form a screen habit. What are our family's rituals and routines? What are the practices in our homes that are just taken for granted? The questions to be asked regarding electronic devices are, "Do I control it or does it control me? Is my will to choose still intact?"

I encourage families to have a family meeting and discuss policies around electronics and screen time. If we don't make conscious choices, forces beyond us will make them for us. We need to teach our kids to be conscious consumers, to make intentional choices in all areas of their lives. "What do I want my life to be like?" This big question begins with the much smaller questions, "What do I want my day to be like? What am I going to spend my time doing?" We are the product of the choices we make. We can let this happen by default, or we can take charge of our lives. And even if we don't choose anything, that in itself is a choice! As Jean-Paul Sartre said, "We are condemned to be free." The measure of a person and the measure of a family is how they use that freedom.

Outside Play

The best alternative to screen time is going outside to play. Have age-appropriate things for the child to do when they go outside. A basketball hoop is one example, but we all know that store-bought activities are never as long-lasting as natural, self-chosen activities like sandboxes, scraps of wood, hoses, and buckets. Adam has piles of scrap wood in his backyard, and he is always hammering. He loves Minecraft but leaves it to work on his real-world houses! Our houses and backyards need to be kid-friendly. Kids on screens don't make messes. Kids off screens make messes. If we don't want them on the screens, we have to be willing to accept their messes. A mess is a sign of a happy, busy child. We have become obsessed with appearances, especially about the tidiness of our homes, and our kids are paying the price. It is no wonder they choose cyberspace over home space. They can do what they want there and make as much of a mess as they want to. They can even blow things up!

Extracurricular Activities

One way of cutting down on screen time is participating in extracurricular activities. We have all heard the warnings about the over-scheduled child, and it's a legitimate concern. Some kids are out every night doing some kind of sport, activity, or program. Parents are sometimes motivated by a sense of competition. I have to give my kid an edge by having them be as good at as many things as possible. Sometimes it's motivated by fear. I have to keep them off the streets. In the age of the screen, extracurricular activities can simply be about bringing variety into a child's life.

My main advice to parents when it comes to choosing extracurricular activities is to follow the lead of the child and go with the child's strengths. We sometimes use extracurriculars as an attempt to "cure" or at least develop an area of weakness. But let's think of ourselves. Think of some activity we would never sign up for. It could be reasoned that it would "do us good" to develop that ability, but we avoid it because we're not good at it or not interested in it. Would we force ourselves to sign up for it anyway? We would likely stick to things we are good at or are interested in developing proficiency at. I recommend the same attitude with children. We see them as blank slates who we can turn into hockey players simply by enrolling them in hockey. It is true that a child may not know what they're interested in until they try, and there are lots of kids who take to something and love it even though they would never have chosen it themselves. But eventually kids reach an age when they have enough experience of themselves to know what they like and what they don't. There are some kids who don't like team sports — that's okay. Some kids are enrolled in something they hate and are forced to continue with it no matter what. It is important to honour a commitment, so I advise parents to agree on a minimum time commitment before signing up. They can't quit as soon as it becomes hard or boring. This is why it is important to have buy-in from the child from the very beginning.

I have worked with many interesting kids and families over the years who have come up with a host of alternative and interesting extra-curricular activities. Here is a partial list. Call it "alternatives to hockey."

- Community theatre productions
- Children's choirs
- Chess club
- Book club
- Art lessons
- Archery
- Historical re-enactments
- Go-cart racing
- Beekeeping
- Volunteering at the animal shelter
- Field trips to any places of personal interest (Ferrari car dealership, Gettysburg battlefield)
- Trade shows (reptile show, collector toy show, comic-book show)

Here's one more option. They can start their own club. A mother I know has a ten-year-old son who loves to do art of all kinds. She got four or five of his friends and cousins together and started an art club. My kids loved to read. We knew lots of other kids who loved to read too. I started a book club at the local library. This club lasted for many years and eventually divided into two clubs based on age — Junior Book Club and Senior Book Club. My wife got together with a group of mothers and organized drama productions. They adapted all kinds of stories, from Dr. Seuss to Shakespeare, for a group of five- to twelve-year-olds. There are lots of spaces available at no charge to non-profit groups in libraries and community centers. How would our culture change if these kinds of activities were more common? Maybe they would eventually draw as many kids as hockey does.

Get Out There and Explore!

It is important for kids to be aware of the world around them. This awareness should always be tied to the child's developmental stage — what they are ready to take in, process, understand, and incorporate into their world view. For infants and toddlers, the world around them comes in through their immediate sense perceptions, and this is more than enough. To quote the English poet William Blake, children "see the world in a grain of sand." When our kids were all under the age of seven, we took them on a hike. My adult goal was to make it to a lake at the end of the trail. We did not make it more than a couple of hundred yards. The kids had to stop and play with every stick and stone they saw. There was enough right in front of them to keep them busy for hours. All that mattered was that they were in nature. The idea of a trail leading somewhere better meant nothing to them. They had already arrived. Earlier I mentioned Richard Louv's term *nature deficit disorder* — a condition affecting kids who do not get enough exposure to nature. For Louv, this deficit explains many of the issues we see in kids today, from inattentiveness to depression. As our kids spend more time on screens, they lose touch with nature. He says, "The future will belong to the nature-smart — those individuals, families, businesses, and political leaders who develop a deeper understanding of the transformative power of the natural world and who balance the virtual with the real. The more high-tech we become, the more nature we need."

As children grow older, they begin to learn that they are part of a larger community. This begins with extended family, moves out to neighbourhood, school, and town and eventually to country and world. It is very important for children to have a sense of place. "Where do I live? Where am I from? What is my immediate world like?" We cannot move confidently through the world if we only know our immediate bubble, our house and street. Eventually, life will require us to go beyond these boundaries. Some kids grow up to be overly cautious about this because they haven't had the early practice in the safe company of Mom and Dad. They have not been gradually guided to a wider world, so when they are thrust into it they respond by withdrawing. Earlier, we discussed the issue of temperament, and identified two aspects of it:

1. Approach or withdrawal: the response to a new object or person, in terms of whether the child accepts the new experience or withdraws from it.
2. Adaptability: the adaptability of behavior to changes in the environment.

A child's temperament is innate but can also be influenced by experience. A child with little exposure to the larger world will be more likely to withdraw and less adaptable to new situations.

In our highly scheduled world, kids are pretty good at approaching new social situations in *kid world* and adapting quickly — daycare, school, after-school programs, summer camps, and sports teams. This is done out of necessity, and it is a priority for busy working parents that the child can be easily dropped off in various settings with little difficulty. But what about places and activities that are more challenging than kid world? I'm thinking of the kinds of activities that are usually done as a family, which gives us the added benefit of letting us bond with children who we don't see enough of and in a completely different way than we do in our day-to-day lives at home.

- Hiking
- Camping
- Attending concerts
- Going to galleries and museums (not as part of a bus load of kids)
- Visiting historic sites
- Exploring interesting parts of one's own town
- Visiting other towns and cities
- Being exposed to other cultures

Beyond the bonding function of these activities and the creation of wonderful family memories, the child is learning to confidently move beyond his or her boundaries, to explore unfamiliar places and things. Eventually, this becomes an attitude toward life generally. "The world is an interesting place to be explored," they learn. "I am capable of trying new things. I can handle new situations." These are very important lessons to instill at an early age. Many kids going off to college or university at the age of seventeen report, "I don't feel ready." This is because their life experience has been so limited. It is a by-product of our overly cautious, protective parenting culture and so much time spent in cyberspace.

Part 4

Boys, Sex, and Relationships

What is it like to live inside a boy's body, and how is that different from living inside a girl's body? The first question can only be answered by a male. The second question can never be answered completely. Any attempt to talk about male experience might be seen as exclusive ("girls experience that too!"). This may be the case, but this book is about what it is like to be a boy, and what do boys need in order to become fully functioning, emotionally healthy men? Their experience of their bodies and their relationship to their bodies are a huge part of this question. The easiest way to describe the male experience of the body is developmentally because the most obvious and powerful reality is that the body is always changing, and the boy is always trying to process and keep up with these changes.

Nowhere does the interplay between nature and nurture reveal itself more clearly than in the male body. Biologically, we are the product of millions of years of evolution. Our bodies have an inherent nature, and they function in particular ways that have evolved for the purposes of adaptation. What is not inherent are the ideas, feelings, and responses boys have to their bodies, to their maleness. These are largely socially constructed — sometimes for good, sometimes not. When we talk about innate male characteristics there is a danger of being deterministic — "because you are male, you will automatically behave in this way, or your nature is fixed in a particular way." It is important to remember that what males are and how they act is the product of biology and culture combined. We have been undergoing a profound sea change in gender roles and gender identity in the past few decades, a process that continues to this day and will have to continue for some time to come. Males need to redefine themselves because of the incredible redefinition that has taken place among women. Men, in short, cannot continue the way they were. This redefinition will entail different child-rearing approaches, which will require mothers and fathers to understand how boys are made — both biologically and socially. We cannot change the biological makeup of the male, but we can change our parenting practices. What needs to be kept and what needs to be let go?

14

Puberty: The Biggest Change in a Boy's Life

Puberty is the key threshold through which each boy must pass on his way to becoming a man. It is a period little talked about by men and boys. Much is left to chance, and much ends up in confusion. On a purely chemical level, testosterone levels rise dramatically causing so many changes in a boy's body that he can feel as though he is becoming another person. Throughout history we have had stories of the man who transforms into something much bigger and stronger. *Beauty and the Beast*, werewolf stories, and superhero stories like *The Incredible Hulk* depict this sudden and overpowering transformation from a mild-mannered man to an aggressive, powerful beast. Boys feel this burgeoning energy in themselves during puberty and their whole relationship to their body changes. Increase in overall size, increased muscle mass, body odour, body hair, acne, and spontaneous erections are among the most noticeable changes. They all have one thing in common — the boy cannot control them. He feels confused and vulnerable to these strong forces acting in his body. The moodiness of puberty is partly hormonal and partly a valid emotional response to what is going on inside.

This traumatic period can lead to feelings of sadness or grief over the loss of the former self. Childhood's end is a deeper theme in men's lives than any of us imagine. The loss of innocence is a profound archetype. One of the stories most deeply embedded in the hard drive of Western civilization is the story of Adam and Eve. Scholars like Joseph Campbell have suggested that the Adam and Eve story is really about the loss of innocence that we all experience — the movement from a harmonious, blissful world where everything is provided and there are no choices to be made (childhood) to a harsh life of struggle, pain, and choice (adulthood). The eating of the apple, which lies at the center of the story, expresses two profound changes in consciousness. First is the introduction of choice, implying free will, consequences, and therefore responsibility for one's actions. The second aspect of the apple story seems to express something particular to the male psyche — the introduction of the feminine "other" as a sexual being. They cover their nakedness, and feminine energy becomes something potentially dangerous. The concept of *temptation* combines both elements — choice and sexuality.

In puberty, when a boy begins to feel a new sense of his physical power, he also begins to think about the use of that power. He thinks about choice, free will, and responsibility. It is a profound existential moment. "Who am I? How should I act?" These two deep questions are linked. "How would a person like me act? How do my actions reveal who I am?" We become self-conscious precisely because we are watching ourselves in order to find out who we are. Those hours spent in front of the mirror or ruminating over how we acted in a particular situation all have a vital purpose. Boys are trying to figure out who they are. They look in the mirror to become accustomed to their new physical body and the new face looking back at them. Boys intensely analyze their behaviour both in the situation and afterwards to figure out who that person doing those actions is. It is as though boys are watching a video of themselves, trying to learn about themselves. Self-consciousness and self-absorption have a valid purpose during puberty. The other mirror boys look into to learn about themselves is how other people respond to them. The child in puberty is intensely interested in this feedback. It appears to get boiled down into acceptance and rejection, but in reality it is far more complex than that. We discover we are funny when people laugh. We discover we are kind when people warm up to us. We discover we are loveable when we are loved. Conversely, we think we are stupid when people laugh at us. We think we are dumb when we fail. We think we are unlovable when we are rejected. Two things boys fear most during this period are humiliation and rejection.

The second aspect of the Adam and Eve story is the transformation of feminine energy into something separate, something desirable yet slightly dangerous. During the process of puberty the androgyny of childhood is lost. The child who exhibited a broad range of behaviours and emotions begins to edit himself. Behaviour gets divided into two categories — masculine and feminine. He narrows the range of what he permits himself to say and do and feel for fear of appearing too feminine, too much like a girl. He achieves a masculine identity by rejecting what he perceives as feminine energy within himself. This is where the greatest damage is done. This is where boys become half-people. The reason so many men suffer in later life, and the reason they visit that suffering on other people, is that they have experienced the great wound of puberty, the splitting off of what is perceived as feminine energy, or, to put it another way, the denial of one's full humanity, one's true nature. Girls face the same crossroads at puberty. "Which aspects of myself will be accepted and which will be rejected? What about myself do I need to deny?" Young girls are now encouraged to hold onto their assertive, logical side. They are permitted a much broader range of behaviour, and we have seen the positive results — women moving into all areas of human endeavour. The same transformation has not happened with boys. They are still encouraged to deny their emotional, creative, nurturing sides. They learn it from their peers, their parents, and their culture. Boys are rough and tough, and they do not show emotion. Emotions are for girls. It is a sad and destructive lesson, and we see the results every day in male depression, aggression, anti-social behaviour, withdrawal (into cyberspace, pornography, sports), and the inability to commit to relationships.

15

Men (and Boys) Are Only Interested in One Thing

Men need what women need — love, affirmation, and connection. Men become cut off from their own needs because of the expectations that develop over time — expectations others have about their needs and the expectations they develop about their own needs — that they don't have any, or that they only need "one thing" (sex). It is a gross distortion of the male psyche, and it has profound implications. While reading several psychological studies of the effects of internet pornography on teenagers, I came across phrases such as "Boys, not surprisingly..." or "Of course boys..." Even academic psychologists who claim to adopt an objective, empirical approach seem to accept it as a given that boys are naturally prone to be preoccupied with sex. I have worked closely with teenage boys for over thirty years, and it is clear to me that boys want the same things girls want — love, affirmation, and connection. To what degree do our social stereotypes about boys create the men we end up with? Boys are subtly trained to ignore their deepest needs and pursue those interests their culture deems acceptable. Even in our fear that boys will be negatively affected by online pornography lies an assumption that this is where they will naturally be drawn. Boys feel these expectations, and come to believe them. Internet pornography might be accused of capitalizing on male hormonal drives, but it is also capitalizing on cultural stereotypes of what men want while, at the same time, reinforcing them.

In *The Irritable Male Syndrome*, Jed Diamond talks about male depression resulting from an inability to express the full range of emotions. He cites the work of psychologist Ronald Levant, who describes how men process feelings.

> Dr. Ronald Levant's research shows that men have developed two primary responses to emotional issues. For vulnerable feelings, including fear, hurt, and shame, he sees men using anger as the "manly" response. For nurturing feelings, including caring, warmth, connectedness, and intimacy, he sees men channeling these feelings through sex.

This process begins in puberty, when boys become both extremely aware of their bodies and disconnected from their bodies. As one teenage girl put it to me, "Boys are not comfortable in their own bodies. Girls stroke each other's hair and hug and touch. Boys don't do this." Boys become extremely conflicted about touch. It is something they find pleasure in but they also fear it — especially from other males. Terry, a young man in his thirties, gave in and spent a day at the spa with his wife. The package included a massage. Terry found himself in a room with several men waiting their turn, and the talk turned to how they hoped they wouldn't get a male masseur. Men become suspicious of touch because it becomes equated with power and control — their need to stay in control and not give in to feelings of vulnerability and the need for nurturance. These needs are simply denied. Thoughts and feelings about one's own body get channelled into two main outlets: sex (alone or with another) and working on the body — muscles, strength, and weight.

Internet Pornography

What are boys interested in? The answer to that question is as varied as boys, but by adolescence many boys abandon their true interests in favour of culturally dictated ones — sports, sex, gaming, drugs, and alcohol. At a time when social acceptance by the peer group becomes all-important, the peer group adopts a collective value system prescribed by corporate interests — among them online pornography companies, the largest revenue generators on the internet. I have great respect for those fringy kids who are interested in things of their own choosing. We have labels for these kids like geek and nerd — pejorative labels that mean someone is not following the dictates of the herd. These kids give me hope for humanity and especially for males. If they are able to hold onto their true selves in adolescence, they might be able to do it as adults.

For most boys, any socially sanctioned knowledge they have about sex and their bodies comes from health class. Here the biological changes in the body are listed. In some cases there will be talk about the emotional changes. Diagrams are labelled and columns are matched. There used to be a kind of folklore that every father would take his son aside and give him "the talk" about "the birds and the bees." This seldom happened, or if it did, it more commonly took the form of a question ("Is there anything you need to know?") or an offer ("If you ever have any questions, you can ask me"). Few boys asked, and few fathers continued the conversation. Before the internet, boys got most of their information from "the street" which meant friends, older kids, and magazines. In the age of the internet our relationship to sex, the body, intimacy, connection, and love have all undergone a profound change. This change is so recent, we do not even know what its effects have been yet. Any boy born after 1995 (the year the internet became widely accessible) has grown up in a radically different world from the one his parents grew up in. Psychologists are just beginning to study the effects of the internet and few conclusions have yet to be drawn.

On a purely practical level, any question a boy has can be answered instantly on the internet; any curiosity can be instantly satisfied — in graphic detail. In many ways this is a good thing, but we must ask ourselves two questions: What kind of sex is portrayed in pornography, and what are children (and people generally) capable of processing? Our minds and bodies, our perceptual systems, are designed for direct experience. We take the world in through our five senses. In cyberspace, one sense predominates — the sense of sight. But the intensity and variety of images surpasses anything we would see in real life. This is true of the internet generally, but it is especially true of internet pornography — a place many boys go to satisfy their curiosity. What they see there is far beyond what the central nervous system of the human being was designed to be able to process, and it only comes in through one doorway — sight. There is no talking or touching or listening — only seeing. Researchers have found that the sense of sight may be the most powerful sense when it comes to making an impression on the brain. Owens, Behun, Manning, and Reid, in "The Impact of Internet Pornography on Adolescents: A Review of the Research," report that:

> research in the field of information processing also provides insight into how pictorial stimuli such as pornography may be encoded in cortical regions in a more indelible manner when compared to other stimuli.... This effect, known as the picture-superiority effect, has been well established in adults and more recently, evidence for this phenomenon has been found in a study of adolescents.... The essential notion of this phenomenon is that greater levels of cortical processing and encoding occur, which favor recognition and retention of pictures over other stimuli such as spoken words.... Although the mechanisms of action for this effect are unclear and likely differ based on the salience of the stimuli..., it is likely that pornographic images are processed differently by the brain and leave a deeper impression compared to verbal or word stimuli. Subsequently, it is important to note that adolescents may process pictorial images quite differently than they do other stimuli, which may have lasting implications for the field of sexual education.

This information is particularly relevant for boys, for whom sight is the most developed and most active sense of perception. The images of pornography can become imprinted in the male mind in an indelible way, especially when they are combined with such powerful emotional and hormonal associations. In short, what boys see stays with them.

"I know it's not good for me, but I watch it anyway." Pornography is an artificial stimulant. Nowhere in nature do we see animals watching other animals have sex in order to become aroused, and at no time in history was it considered natural to watch other couples have sex. Erotic art and the depiction of the naked body is a completely different thing, and has existed since art began. Researchers tell us pornography creates a dopamine rush that is pleasure-inducing such that the brain seeks it out again, but the more this rush is induced artificially, the less it is able to happen naturally. Heavy users of pornography report a reduced sex drive and a lack of interest in real-world sex, saying they can only achieve the same level of arousal with internet pornography, which is more focused, more intense, and completely self-directed. Research also shows that heavy users of pornography become unable to get the same "high" from conventional pornography and are eventually drawn to depictions of more unconventional, fringe, and socially abhorrent sexual practices.

In surveys, one of the reasons males report for using pornography is that it "teaches them what to do." We need to be concerned about pornography because of the lessons it teaches implicitly and explicitly. The relationships depicted in pornography are superficial and mechanical. There is no commitment, no true connection. In fact, many images depict women in a degraded role with the man (or several men) in the role of aggressor. Owens, Behun, Manning, and Reid tell us that "consistent findings have emerged linking adolescent use of pornography that depicts violence with increased degrees of sexually aggressive behavior."

Rape Culture

The term *rape culture* has been coined to describe what appears to be a pervasive attitude among males about what is acceptable and what is not in sexual relations. If there is a rape culture, it originated in internet pornography where depictions of forced sex are ubiquitous. This phenomenon has occurred simultaneously with the sexualization of our culture through advertising, movies, and television. We are all victims of this situation because we are so powerless to control it. Corporate interests have latched onto a deep human impulse and exploit it daily for profit. Sex has become an underlying pervasive presence in our culture. American writer Pamela Paul has described this in detail in her critically acclaimed book *Pornified: How Pornography Is Damaging Our Lives, Our Relationships, and Our Families.*

The implications for boys are particularly profound. When boys become the product of a sexualized, pornographic culture, girls suffer, and boys themselves suffer. They are both robbed of the happiness and fulfillment that come from emotionally healthy human relationships. Both women's and men's lives can be destroyed by sexual violence. There have been numerous stories in the press of women coming forward to describe sexual assault in the dating situation long after the fact. The Twitter hashtag *#beenrapedneverreported*, initiated by *Montreal Gazette* reporter Sue Montgomery, became an international phenomenon. One reason women don't report is compassion and a sense of human decency that makes them unwilling to subject another person to the public humiliation of charges. The question arises then, why do some men not feel this same sense of compassion and human decency in the bedroom? In addition to the influence of a pornographic culture, what is it about the way we raise boys that allows certain men to turn off any feeling of empathy for the woman they are with?

Males will sometimes blame the girl for being too seductive, or the influence of alcohol. This is a childish attempt to deflect responsibility. Men have free will to the same degree that women do. The disgusting stereotype that men "think with their penises" has got to be erased. Men and women are both victims of this stereotype. When the only solutions are pepper spray or the courts, then men have been reduced to the level of predatory animals or criminals. Women are coming out of the shadows to talk about their experiences. Men need to talk too. We see young women being supported and guided by older women, many of whom have been through the same thing. We do not see the same with men. Young men need to be guided and supported by older men to a healthier form of sexuality.

Campus Life: Kids Only

We have heard in the news that *rape culture* is particularly a problem on many university and college campuses in North America. When one visits a college dorm, one of the things that stands out is the absence of older adults. It is a community of young men and women (some who are still teenagers), products of a sexualized, pornographic culture, at the height of their own biological fertility. Alcohol is a given. There are no authority figures present among a group of people who have spent the previous eighteen years of their lives being controlled by external forces at home and at school. They have never been required to practise self-regulation, so they are totally unprepared to do so here. Brain research tells us that the impulse control center in the frontal lobe develops later in males than it does in females. All of these factors combine to create a situation where problems are bound to occur and mistakes are bound to be made. As elders, we do nothing to anticipate or manage this situation. We leave our children to their own devices and then condemn them in shock when they "mess up."

I am not suggesting that we need older adults on campus to act as watch dogs, to continue the helicopter parenting/teaching that caused the problem in the first place. What these young people need is age-mixing. Throughout the developmental stages, we look to those older than us for a model of what's next. I have talked about the import-ance of age-mixing in elementary and high schools where peer men-toring can be so powerful. The same thing is needed in post-secondary institutions. Proximity to and interaction with older adults provides practice for the next stage in one's development.

Why are there no older adults living in close proximity to young people on our university campuses? Youth culture has become what writer Ariel Levi calls *raunch culture*. It is not a particularly pleasant culture to be in for mature adults, nor for young people — particularly for sensitive, intelligent, highly accomplished young people. Why then do we allow this raunch culture to take over by default? Why is no attempt made to create a more positive culture in the microcosm of academia? Why is such a suggestion seen as conservative or stodgy? Because the voice of raunch culture tells us so. We need to talk back to youth culture or raunch culture; otherwise, we are left with a world where kids are raising kids and the only moral compass young people have to use is the one handed to them by popular culture.

Restorative Justice

Restorative justice needs to be a more common approach in highly nu-anced date-rape cases. No one benefits from the judicial approach to these problems. Women are re-traumatized by the process of coming forward, and young men's careers and reputations can be ruined for life. Both sides end up angry, hurt, and confused. No one comes out healed or satisfied. Any talk of sympathy for the male perpetrator is often met with outrage. We want the man to pay. What does this mean? Public humiliation? Incarceration? What does the individual woman want? In most cases, she does not want to destroy him. She wants the man to know how this affected her. She wants him to understand and admit that it was wrong. She wants remorse. She wants an apology. She wants to be sure that no other woman will go through what she did. She wants to know that the man has changed.

A male who wants to apologize, who wants to talk about what happened, who needs to talk about what happened, is not able to because of the adversarial nature of the system. If a male tries to discuss the details of the moment, the complex chemistry of the situation, he is shut down. There is no learning or growth. He may retreat into an even more entrenched misogynistic position. He must immediately go into defence mode. He cannot admit any wrongdoing. The current system is completely black and white. A person's either guilty or they're innocent. This does not do justice to the complex reality of the situation.

What is meant by restorative justice? The following definition appears on the website of Correctional Service Canada:

> In the face of crime and conflict, restorative justice (RJ) is a philosophy and an approach that views crime and conflict principally as harm done to people and relationships. It strives to provide support and safe opportunities for the voluntary participation and communication between those affected (victims, offenders, and community) to encourage accountability, reparation, and a movement towards understanding, feelings of satisfaction, healing, safety, and a sense of closure. RJ is a non-adversarial, non-retributive approach to justice that emphasizes healing in victims, meaningful accountability of offenders, and the involvement of citizens in creating healthier, safer communities.

This approach to "harm done to people and relationships" must become more common. We need to evolve beyond our primitive eye-for-an-eye logic. We also need to abandon the medieval practice of public humiliation as a form of punishment. Our courts have become the pillory complete with an angry mob and an accompanying media circus. If we were to use restorative justice more, and if we were to pay attention to what was being said on all sides, we would produce a body of knowledge and understanding that could transform the cultural roots of these problems. In order to understand how something works, we have to take it apart and examine it closely. We could discover the root causes of misogyny and violence if we had the courage to look at them objectively. The current adversarial system of attack and defend does not lead to any kind of understanding or enlightenment.

What Can We Do as Parents About Online Pornography?

Unfortunately, a child's first exposure to pornography is usually accidental. For the sexually immature or highly sensitive child, it could be quite disturbing, even traumatizing. There is an emerging body of research to show that early exposure to pornography can influence later sexual behaviour and attitudes toward sex and women, but there is little information on the confusion, anxiety, and depression these images can cause. Children have a particular view of the adult world. They idealize their parents, teachers, and other authority figures. Most children are open and comfortable with physical expressions of affection and even romantic love, but pornographic images present a different kind of emotional world, one where the physical aspect of actions completely replaces or degrades the emotional dimension. A child can see pornography is not about love, caring, connection, or commitment. It separates the personal from the physical. This is disturbing to a child for whom all physical expression is a product of interior feeling. For children, the body and the heart are connected. Pornography separates the body from the heart. It is about physical pleasure alone. Adults are a child's primary caregivers, world-definers, and role models. "Is this what adults do? Is this what Mom and Dad do? Is this natural?" These are the questions boys ask. With only the internet to guide them, the answer is yes.

While electronic devices open up the world for us, they are also a bit like Pandora's boxes in that they contain a lot of toxic material that, once released, cannot be put back in. Once a child stumbles across pornography or seeks it out, the images can have an indelible influence. It is important to talk to kids about this possibility. The language we use depends on the age and awareness of the child. Explain that the internet is a place where all people go — children as well as adults — so they might see some things that are not meant for children. "If you see something that you find confusing or don't like, then don't look at it. You are always free to choose what to look at and what not to look at." While this might sound simplistic, it is a fundamentally important lesson for this passive medium. Just because something is on the screen, doesn't mean one has to look at it. A good example are the ads that come on at the start of YouTube videos where the viewer is given a countdown and is able to skip the ad in three seconds. In clicking *skip* we are practising *not looking*. This is a valid, indeed important, skill to learn on the internet.

What we don't want to say is that pictures of bodies, certain parts of the body, or naked people are bad. I used to have a copy of Botticelli's great Renaissance painting *The Birth of Venus* in my classroom. It depicts a naked Venus with one breast exposed. More than one grade nine boy commented on it. "Sir, are you allowed to have that in the room?" or "Sir, do you think that picture is appropriate?" This is the sad side effect of our sexualized culture, but it is also the result of our confused response to a pornographic culture. In condemning sexual explicitness of any kind, we end up condemning many other things by association. Naked bodies become inappropriate. Breasts become objects of shame. A lot of kids who look at classical art feel confused. Why are all these people naked? They cannot conceive of a culture in which the body was celebrated as the highest form of beauty. Today, the body has become an object of sexual stimulation as well as an object of shame — only to be looked at in the secret solitude of the screen. We need to teach our kids about this distinction, that there are many ways of looking at the body and sex. They are both wonderful, beautiful things. The body is good. Feel it. Use it. Enjoy it. Listen to it. Some people have taken the body and sex and used them in negative ways. We have the power to choose which attitude we want to adopt. We begin with what we choose to look at. This might sound prudish or puritanical, but we say the same thing about food. We choose what we put into our mouths. We say we need to make wise food choices. The same is true of the images we consume. If we are what we eat, then we are what we pay attention to. Junk food tastes good, but harms our health. Junk images (like pornography) make us feel good, but harm our emotional health. As kids get older they should be led through this same kind of analysis. What is wrong with pornography? Does it promote healthier human relationships, or does it alienate people from each other? Does it make people happier or more dissatisfied?

The kind of relationship and communication style we have with our children is the foundation for dealing with all the problems life will bring — the internet being only one of them. If we are open and comfortable with any topic, our children will be. If our children know we trust and respect them, they will be willing to share things with us. On a more practical level, here is a list of strategies that can be implemented immediately:

1. Keep the family computer in a high-traffic area or be around when kids are using a tablet. This applies mainly to families of young children where there is still only one family screen. Once screens proliferate throughout the house, monitoring becomes much harder.

2. Install a filter on the family computer. We can also enable restrictions on an iPhone, iPad, or iPod touch and set up parental controls on an android device.

3. Install parental control apps that allow filtering of adult content, setting of time limits, and monitoring of the child's internet activity.

4. Do not allow screens at bedtime.

5. Do not have data plans on a child's phone. If the cell phone is for safety and convenience to contact Mom and Dad (a reasonable thing), there is no need to be surfing the net.

6. Have a specific family policy around screen use and the consequences for violation of the rules. Enforce these policies firmly, fairly, and consistently.

One caution: some of the strategies above imply distrust. People become what they are perceived to be. We do not want to degenerate into cat-and-mouse parenting where we are trying to "catch our child being bad." We do not want to become spies or policemen to our child. If our child feels we don't trust them or if they know we will overreact to situations, they will be far less likely to come to us with issues, and they will learn to hide what they are doing. Always err on the side of trust. If the trust is violated, discuss it and impose proportional consequences; however, we have no choice but to push the reset button on trust.

The healthy response to sexual curiosity is not to shut it down, deny it, and be on constant guard for signs of transgression. We can end up labelling too many things as inappropriate. Whenever we use the word *inappropriate*, we must ask ourselves two important questions: Inappropriate to whom, and inappropriate according to what yardstick? Are we applying the judgment criteria of intelligent, emotionally healthy adults or simplistic thinking originating in emotionally unhealthy attitudes? Sexual curiosity is like all human curiosity. It is how we learn, and it gives us pleasure to find things out. Let's not pour unnecessary water over that fire.

Parents who have a conflicted, suspicious, or inhibited attitude toward sex, touch, and pleasure pass this on to their children. These children become confused about sensual experience. They become less able to distinguish between good touch and bad touch, seeing all touch as suspect. Sex, pleasure, and touch then get pushed underground. They become deformed versions of what they are naturally intended to be, and sound judgments about these distorted versions become hard to make for those who live in this shadow world. The child who has grown up in a shadow world of sexual attitudes is more likely to find his distorted emotional world reflected in online pornography. The commonly tread path for these children is the path to greater emotional confusion, repression, and a general stifling of real-world sensual life.

Children who grow up with a relaxed, open, positive attitude toward sex, pleasure, and touch are less susceptible to the shadow world of online pornography because when they meet it, they see it for what it is — limited, stifling, neurotic, and unhappy. It is not the world of the senses they have known. It turns them off. They turn away from it — naturally.

16

Boys and Gender Identification

In the past few decades a whole new area of academic study has opened up — gender studies. It began with feminism and women's studies and has expanded to include both genders, but more importantly, it has shown us that gender is actually much more complex than we originally thought. Gender can be broken down into a number of facets:

- Assigned gender (determined by genitals at birth)
- Gender identity (one's subjective perception of their own gender)
- Gender preference (the gender one is erotically attracted to)
- Gender roles (behaviours and roles taught by one's culture)
- Gender expression (how one acts)

The interplay between these elements can become quite complicated. Joe was born a boy (assigned gender), yet from a very early age felt himself to be a girl (gender identification). In his early twenties he underwent the medical process to transition to a female body (gender reassignment surgery). His gender preference before surgery and hormonal therapy was for females and remained so after he transitioned. He would smile when whistled at by men on the street in whom he had no interest. His gender expression had both traditionally feminine and masculine traits. He (now she) enjoys her makeup, long hair, and high heels but also loves trucks, motorcycles, and working in construction.

Governments and other institutions are in the process of learning about and accommodating a wide range of gender-related issues under pressure from human rights organizations, the courts, and people who identify in these various ways. The Ontario Ministry of Education, in its *Accepting Schools Act* of 2012, stated:

> The people of Ontario and the Legislative Assembly … believe that students need to be equipped with the knowledge, skills, attitudes, and values to engage the world and others critically, which means developing a critical consciousness that allows them to take action on making their schools and communities more equitable and inclusive for all people, including LGBTTIQ (lesbian, gay, bisexual, transgender, transsexual, two-spirited, intersex, queer, and questioning) people.

It is a sign of the times to see such a lexicon included in a document from one of the most conservative arbiters of the status quo.

Norrie May-Welby was born a boy in Scotland, underwent gender reassignment surgery at the age of twenty-three, but now identifies as neutral. She petitioned the Australian Human Rights Commission, and after a four-year battle, the High Court ruled that her official documents could be designated "sex not specified." Norrie has been called the first "sexless" person in the world, but we must ask ourselves if this is, indeed, the best label. Norrie is really the first person to defy self-definition in terms of the dual categories of male and female. Perhaps gender doesn't even exist along a continuum of male to female. Perhaps it is much more complex — a web of many thoughts, feelings, attitudes, and behaviours with a human being at the center.

We are more aware than ever before of the social construction of gender, the nature-versus-nurture debate, and the fact that little boys' and girls' attitudes about themselves and each other are hugely influenced by the way they are socialized. At the same time there has been an explosion of research into innate biological differences between male and female brains. Evolutionary biology and evolutionary psychology have shown us how gender differences have evolved over millennia in response to assigned roles related to survival of the species. And just as we have gained all this information, gender is being reassessed and redefined all around us by individuals who are simply acting on their own courage and self-awareness. Never has the situation been more fluid and never has it been more confusing. However, just because something is confusing doesn't mean it's wrong. Confusion is a prerequisite for wisdom. We are on the threshold of a completely new era in gender roles, gender identification, and gender relations. Our boys are growing up at a time in history when what it means to be a boy or a man is undergoing a profound change not just on the level of gender roles but on the level of gender identification. What is most interesting to contemplate is that we are not inventing new versions of gender. We are simply in the process of normalizing and thereby liberating versions of gender that have probably existed since the beginning of time. We are now simply removing the artificial social constraints and constructs that limited the incredible variety within the human species. The only impediment to this beautiful process will be fear.

Our main concern during this time of unprecedented social transformation should be for those kids who are trying to understand themselves and how they feel in a culture that is very conflicted about the changes going on. As a more open and liberal attitude toward sexual orientation gains ground, the alternative voice criticizing non-traditional sex roles is heard more loudly as well. Both sides are equally passionate about the rightness of their position, so there is no final authority a young person can go to for the "right" answer. It seems to come down to a question of opinion. The voices closest to the child will probably be the most influential.

If a parent applies the following fundamental precepts of good parenting, then any child, gay or straight, from a liberal or a conservative family, should be able to work their way through to a personal understanding of their own nature and a satisfying life:

- Honour the nature of the child
- Listen to the child (no matter what they say)
- Respect the child (even when we do not agree with what they *do*)

- Love the child (unconditionally)
- Trust the child
- Accept the child for who they are
- Do not pass judgment on the child

The list above is written for a secular audience. The same list can be understood from the perspective of any of the major religious traditions of the world.

- All great religious traditions teach that God's creation is ultimately a profound mystery that we do not completely understand. We believe that God is all goodness, and therefore, what God creates must be good. Honour the mysterious nature of the child.
- All great religious traditions teach love of one's neighbour. Our children are our closest neighbours. Under this command fall these parenting principles.
  · Listen to the child (no matter what they say)
  · Respect the child (even when we do not agree with what they *do*)
  · Love the child (unconditionally)
  · Trust the child
- All great religious traditions teach that we should be hesitant in our judgments of others, that ultimately only God can judge. Therefore, even from a religious point of view, we should do the following:
  · Accept the child for who he is
  · Do not pass judgment on the child

The only remaining admonition of the main religious traditions that is not dealt with here is the teaching that evil is present in the world, that we must resist evil and work for good. Homosexuality (in all its forms) is sometimes spoken of as an evil by religious groups. How do we distinguish between good and evil? This question has plagued religious thinkers and philosophers for millennia. One answer comes from these same religious traditions: we judge a tree by the fruit it produces. The condemnation of homosexuality leads to the rejection of homosexual kids. It leads to profound suffering on the part of those kids and those who love them. It can quite often lead to serious emotional and psychological problems and often even death by murder or suicide. If these are the fruits of this "truth," then it is not a valid truth. It is an invalid truth, a constructed truth, that must be driven out of the community as if it were a force for evil itself. An incredible amount of suffering is experienced by kids who are confused, questioning, and searching — with no compassionate voice to guide them. I have witnessed the shocking phenomenon of parents who completely reject their child because of issues around gender. They might reject them emotionally or quite literally throw them out of the house. How can ignorance and fear be so strong that they would compel a parent to such an unnatural act? The child they brought into the world, loved, nurtured, and raised, they now reject! Where does this ignorance and fear originate? Our religious traditions, which speak so much about compassion and mercy, have much to answer for in this regard.

Catholic moral theology, for example, is based on "natural philosophy." Homosexual behaviour is considered *disordered* because nature dictates that the purpose of intercourse is procreation. Since persons of the same sex cannot have intercourse leading to procreation, their sexual expression is considered disordered (or morally wrong). What we are faced with is the need for a re-examination of what is "natural." We used to believe that the sun revolved around the earth. Now we know that the earth revolves around the sun. In other words, we replaced one truth about natural law with a truer truth about what is natural. In the same way, we are moving toward a truer truth about gender. History shows us two things: that change is inevitable, and that humans do not deal well with change. There has always been tension between those who would like to keep things the way they have always been and those who would like to evolve in new directions. It took the Catholic Church centuries to admit that Galileo was right. Sadly, we cannot always look to our most revered institutions for truth. In terms of gender redefinition, there are still many who cling to the belief that the sun revolves around the earth: that a man is a man, a woman is a woman, and heterosexual marriage is the only valid life. Change will take time, but change is inevitable.

When a child who is gay is raised with love and acceptance, they grow up to be strong, healthy, happy members of society who contribute in all the ways we expect any person to. They bring love to the world and enrich it with their own unique nature. Nature abhors a monoculture. It seems to abhor a dual culture too. One way of being a man and one way of being a woman is not enough for nature (or God, it would seem, to put it in spiritual terms). The evidence is right in front of us.

How to Talk to Boys About Sex

- It's important that we show, starting when children are young, that we are comfortable with whatever topics they might raise. Where there may have been some things in our families of origin that "we just don't talk about," we need to change that program. A child should be free to raise any topic at any time. This is how they learn — by following the natural lead of their curiosity and their thought processes. Our job is to facilitate this at every turn.
- Take your lead from the child. We do not have to raise topics because we think they are important or relevant. If we think a topic might be on a child's mind, we can bring it up, but if the child shows no interest in pursuing it, then we should leave it alone.
- Use clear, concrete language. It's okay to use words like penis, vagina, and breast. Do not use euphemisms like "wee wee" for penis, or "down below" for the genital area.
- We must guard against any shameful tone in our talk about sex and the body. Whispering the names of certain body parts or using words like *dirty* and *bad* create an emotional tone than can become attached to sex, the body, and touch for the rest of a person's life.
- Many little boys like to touch their penises. It is a self-comforting behaviour. We don't need to shame them out of it. We can simply tell them not to do it in public places. They will grow out of it as they become more aware of social norms.

- Younger boys (pre-puberty) usually have a closer verbal rapport with their mothers, so it is perfectly natural that they will probably ask their first questions of her. They do not need to be referred on to Dad. The mother can answer.
- During the teen years (after puberty) boys are less likely to talk to Mom about topics concerning sex or their bodies generally. This is the time for Dad to be aware and available and open to whatever topics may arise (or be lying below the surface).
- Sexual curiosity may lead to sexual exploration and experimentation. For younger children this is natural behaviour and needs to be treated gently. There is no need for shaming. Questions can be answered by the many good children's books about sex and puberty. Curiosity is a positive and natural tendency in children. It is good that they are exercising it, but we must also teach the importance of boundaries.
- In puberty sexual curiosity is often satisfied on the internet. This also needs to be treated gently but seriously. Internet pornography has become a powerful influence on social norms. It is educational whether we like what it teaches or not. The power relations depicted in most pornography are not healthy. The female in pornography is often in a submissive role and all too often in a degraded role. The male is in complete control. He shows little interest in the other person. Physical satisfaction is the goal, not emotional connection. We need to talk to our boys about this.
- In puberty sexual exploration and experimentation can become complicated when the boy feels a sexual attraction or even just erotic interest in the same sex. This may be rooted in simple curiosity. Is he made the same way I am? Does his body work the same way mine does? What are other male bodies like? This sexual curiosity can lead to exploration and experimentation with peers or, in the age of the internet, it can lead to viewing gay pornography. This is more common

than we might expect, and many boys end up feeling a great sense of guilt about it or fear that it means they might be gay or simply "not normal." Many boys pass through a period of confusion about gender preference. They begin with an exploration of the male body (which is more familiar to them) before moving on (or not) to the female body with all its differences and mysteries.

As adults we sometimes feel that if we don't talk about something it won't happen, and if we do talk about something, it will happen. We are afraid that if we talk about something then we will be seen as condoning the behaviour. It is hard to fit the kinds of topics listed above into casual conversation, but they could be incorporated into larger conversations about society, sex, gender, media, or technology. A parent can frame the conversation in a way that is not directed at the child or trying to solicit information from the child. "I was reading this book about boys, and the author said that sometimes boys think they might be gay just because they are curious about other boys' bodies. He said this was normal and boys shouldn't worry about it. I thought that was interesting." This last sentence just puts it out there as something the parent is thinking about. The boy is not required to respond, and just because he doesn't respond doesn't mean he's not listening and might not benefit from the information. If the time is right and the planets are in the right alignment, he may even pick up the topic and develop it further. We can never tell, and we should not try to control such conversations too much.

17

Sexual Abuse: When Children Become Objects

Child sexual abuse (indeed, child abuse of any kind) depends upon seeing the child as an object. It is also rooted in the attitude of entitlement to power that we implicitly teach ourselves to have over children. We do not always see children as autonomous beings deserving of our respect. They become objects to control. It could be argued that the stereotypical Victorian phrase "children should be seen and not heard" is still believed today. In many homes, children are not listened to, and teenagers are "shut down" when they talk back to their parents. Talking back is code for not agreeing with the parent. As patriarchy crumbles and social media gives everyone a voice, "Don't talk back" makes less and less sense to young people. Another cliché that is still believed even though it might not be spoken aloud is the old chestnut "as long as you live under my roof, you'll do what I say." I am the boss, the landlord, the jailer. These are the sad metaphors implied. Children can also come to be seen as property we own or possessions we display.

This objectification of children can be found within the institution of the family and many of our other social institutions as well. School is our primary institution for forming the minds of children. It takes the following ideas as starting points: Children become students. They become the property of the school during school hours. They are units to be managed externally. Their individual wills are secondary to the will of authority. These attitudes lead the child to see himself as a passive recipient of adult behaviour. This can be a dangerous attitude when the adult does not have the best interests of the child at heart. Our children will have to learn to talk back to many voices in their lives. They will have to learn to stand up for themselves. They need to be able to read a situation and make their own good judgments about it. These are hard lessons to learn in the top-down, authoritarian world of school. I worked in several schools as staff advisor to the student council. The teenagers on these councils were among the most mature, responsible, intelligent kids I have ever met. Sometimes they would ask their teachers to be excused from class to help out with a student-run event. They would sometimes be told no, and on more than one occasion the teacher was quoted as saying, "You're mine right now." These words reveal an attitude that permeates our schools.

Most sexual abuse situations involve a power imbalance. This imbalance is amplified by the way we socialize kids to accept adult power unquestioningly. Most people outside of school do not realize how little the will of the child is valued there — in fact, how it is actively discouraged. Parents hand over complete control of their child to the school. Even the parent's will is not valued, and their involvement is actively discouraged except in the most superficial ways. The three rules of school are sit still, be quiet, and do what you're told. These are not helpful rules if we want to teach a child to set clear personal boundaries, be able to talk back, and keep himself safe.

As parents and teachers, we must begin with the assumption that the child is an autonomous being capable of forming his or her own judgments and acting on those judgments. Freedom and responsibility must become the foundation of our parenting and our pedagogical practices. We must begin to work on the assumption that a child is wise and always free to decide what he will or will not do, that a child can say no, and that a child can talk back. We must teach this sense of personal power and autonomy from an early age — with adults and institutions. The days of unquestioning obedience must come to an end. Children must be able to see the legitimacy of authority — authority that is kind and respectful, and that has their best interests at heart.

To those who see children as objects to be managed and controlled, this will appear to be a very liberal, permissive approach with weak boundaries. Sometimes school is just reproducing the attitude toward children found in many homes. The teacher simply continues the parental voice demanding unquestioning obedience to authority. Teachers replace the parents as controllers. When children are respected for their ability to set their own boundaries, some adults can feel very threatened by this. "This is my student, my child, my property. I'm in charge of the child's life." The child is left unable to form his own judgments and is assigned a passive role. His perceptions are not valued.

What We Don't Teach Kids

We used to teach "good touch, bad touch." We taught that some touch is bonding, nurturing, and positive, while other kinds of touch are physically or emotionally hurtful. This required the child to learn to interpret situations for himself and take autonomous action in response to those situations. Now we teach "no touch" — a policy that implies that all touch is bad. It also gives adults the power to decide. We take away the opportunity for children to learn about the range of human behaviour, how to interpret it, and how to respond to it. We do not trust the child to decide, and so they never learn to form their own judgments about what's appropriate and what's not. This is not healthy training for life.

It should not be a surprise that there is so much confusion over the issue of mutual consent. We have raised a generation to do what they're told without any training or trust in their ability to negotiate complex human interactions at a young age. We hear about a rape culture among young males, and about women who do not report sexual assault. One of the reasons might be this early training — or lack of training — to trust one's own judgment, and to act on it. When a young male shows no regard for the feelings of his partner, there may be three possible causes at work. First, the pedagogy of pornography teaches that all women are passive objects and the purpose of sex is male pleasure only. Second, the lack of real-life training he received in a "no touch" childhood. The third cause may be the training he did receive at school where one person got to decide everything, and if the child doesn't like what's happening, too bad. He's not allowed to talk back, and even if he does, he isn't listened to. Similarly, the woman who accepts abuse from her trusted partner must have learned that somewhere — to sit still, be quiet, and do what she's told. We will not stop sexual abuse until we teach kids their rights from an early age — including their right to talk back, and including their right to say what they want and what they don't want. It is a question of boundaries. We teach children boundaries by allowing *them* to set them, and then by respecting them.

What We Should Teach Kids

We talk about *street proofing* our children as though all the threats lie "out there" somewhere. Statistics show that most sexual abuse happens between people who know each other. Experts also tell us that one of the distinguishing characteristics of sexual abuse is an imbalance of power between the two parties. We have been talking about the power imbalance experienced by children in our homes and schools. In order to safeguard them against abuse of all kinds, we must teach our children the important principles we have been discussing throughout this book:

- You always deserve to be respected
- You always deserve to be listened to
- It is important to listen to yourself and to trust your own judgment
- You do not have to do anything you don't feel right about
- It is okay to talk back
- It is okay to stick up for yourself when you don't like what's happening
- It's okay to say negative things about adults

As mentioned earlier, we don't always teach these lessons to our kids because we feel such messages would erode our power over them. We need to let go of that need for power and control. Kids, today more than ever, need to feel a sense of power and control over their own lives and their own bodies, and it starts with our parenting pedagogy. Children who are commanded to always do what they are told and never to talk back will be more vulnerable to abuse. Children need to practise expressing their true feelings with us and having those true feelings validated, so that when they meet someone who denies those feelings and tries to manipulate them, they will see this for what it is — something they are not used to, something that is not healthy. "That's not the way Mom and Dad treat me. I am respected at home. I expect to be respected in other situations as well, and I will walk away or speak up if I feel I am not."

Child-to-Child Sexual Abuse

Sexual exploration and experimentation are common and natural among children. It becomes more complicated when there is a significant age difference between the children involved. At a certain point it meets the criteria for sexual abuse because of the power imbalance created by the age difference. Sometimes an adolescent boy will turn to a younger child to satisfy his curiosity or express sexual feelings. Some researchers have suggested that the children who do this kind of thing with younger children were likely themselves exposed to sexual experiences at an early age, that it is a kind of learned behaviour or a response to one's own exposure. Because these situations are so sensitive and complex, the best way to discuss them is within the context of particular cases. I was involved in two cases that taught me an incredible amount.

David and John

David was in grade ten when he was diagnosed with clinical depression. He was a highly sensitive, intellectually gifted student. Within a month or two of starting the school year, he became unable to attend classes. He cried often and suffered from debilitating anxiety. He disclosed to me that when he was ten years old a twelve-year-old boy, John, had abused him sexually. The parents of the two boys were long-time friends, and the boys had grown up together. They commonly played alone together while the parents socialized. The abuse involved oral sex and attempted anal intercourse. These episodes went on for a couple of months. As teenagers, their interactions became less frequent as the families drifted apart. When David was in grade ten, John was in grade twelve at the same school. David wanted to speak to John before he left high school as he felt he might lose track of him and never be able to have the conversation he wanted to have. Arrangements were made through a local child and family resource center, and David asked if I could mediate this meeting. Originally the school chaplain and a counsellor from the centre were to be there, but we decided the fewer people the better. I knew David very well, and John knew of me and seemed to trust me. When I invited John and told him what the meeting would involve, he was sheepish but completely willing to participate. There was almost a sense of relief in his voice, as though he had somehow been expecting or wanting this opportunity. Before we met, David wrote down what he wanted to say. His anxiety made speaking very difficult for him at the best of times. He knew that it would be hard to express himself in this stressful situation.

The two boys sat across from each other at a round table, and I sat between them although closer to David, who sometimes needed reassurance. John was obviously very embarrassed and stressed, but he was also extremely compassionate. He was completely willing to talk about whatever David wanted to bring up. David had some pointed questions, and John answered them honestly. David's healing was also John's healing. It became clear that John was experiencing a great deal of suffering about what he had done, but he had never had any outlet to express or deal with his guilt and shame. John apologized to David. David wanted to know why John had done it. He wanted to verify particular memories he had of the events, and he wanted John to know how negatively this had affected him. David had trusted John and looked up to him. This is what made it so hard. David didn't want anything bad to happen to John. He made a point of including in his notes that he didn't want John to hurt himself after this conversation. He also told John that he had waited until after John's sixteenth birthday to disclose his name so that the adults involved would not be required to contact Children's Aid or the police. Beneath all the pain and suffering, the humanity of both boys was powerfully evident.

It was clear that John was filled with remorse for what he had done and felt powerless that he couldn't undo it. We don't often think of the suffering of the perpetrator. We might imagine them as someone who is secretly laughing to themselves because they got away with something.

This was not the case with John, and I don't think it's the case with many. We talk easily about helping victims, but we are not very willing to talk about helping perpetrators. They only have our contempt, and so they become the monsters we imagine them to be — distorted versions of themselves, unable to find any kind of resolution to the guilt and pain they feel about what they have done, not to mention any kind of resolution to the problems that caused them to behave this way in the first place. John was a sensitive, lonely boy going through puberty. He confessed that he found David attractive, and that he was full of strong sexual feelings at that time. He had worried that he might be a pedophile, but he had gone on to have several girlfriends as a teenager. One could tell that the worry and self-contempt were still there. From what I knew of both families, the kids were usually left to their own devices. David's parents had major marital and mental health problems. I don't know much about John's parents other than that during these social get-togethers there would be lots of drinking, and the kids would be left alone.

What comes out in this story is the theme of kids on their own trying to deal with strong feelings. For David, feelings of love and admiration for an older boy. For John, similar feelings of love and attraction combined with newly awakening sexual feelings. The other theme that stands out is kids with unmet needs. In both boys I think there was a real need for love, affirmation, connection, and affection. Both boys were looking for something, and they found it, as the saying goes, in the wrong places. Looking for warmth, they were burned by the fire. It is a hard wound to heal, but it is important to understand the dynamic that led to it in order to prevent it from happening to others and also to prevent the quick reflex of moral judgment and condemnation. These were not bad kids. They needed adults to keep an eye out, to be involved, and to provide positive opportunities for the two boys to bond in the way they both wanted to and in a way that was age-appropriate. They also needed time and attention from their parents.

Our default mechanism when it comes to abuse is shame, blame, and punishment. We see this phenomenon in the bullying situation (of which child-to-child sexual abuse can be a form). The student who bullies throughout elementary school will likely go on to bully in high school. We seldom attempt to get at root causes. The punishments inflicted on the bully only reinforce his negative attitude about himself and others. They make him more angry and hostile. The same is true for those whose transgressions are secret and subtle — like John's. He needed to know the results of his actions; he needed to face his victim and he needed to be able to say he was sorry.

Julie and Her Brother: Inter-Sibling Abuse

One of the most common and perhaps most under-reported forms of child sexual abuse is inter-sibling abuse. Julie ended up in an adolescent psychiatric ward after she tried to take her own life near the end of grade eleven. From when she was four to when she was eight, her older brother, who was between ten and fourteen during this time, took advantage of her on several occasions by initiating mutual touching of genitals and engaging in rudimentary forms of oral sex. These episodes always occurred in a surreptitious, covert atmosphere. "He would pretend he was sleeping," she said. The only time Julie could remember one of her parents being remotely involved was a time when her father called down the stairs, "What are you guys doing?" at which point her brother hopped off the couch onto the floor. Julie would go back to that moment as proof that *she* had been in the wrong, "I must have known it was wrong." She could not bring herself to feel the same intensity of blame for her brother or her father that she felt for herself.

Julie looked up to her older brother. She would do anything to win his favour. He saw her as an irritating little sister. There was not much respect and there were very poor boundaries. "He was mean to me at other times. I was so happy he was showing attention to me. I just wanted to be his friend." Behind these troubling events lie the strong emotions that fuel them, emotions that find no other outlet. Eventually the abuse came to an end, but the damage had been done and Julie was left to deal with her emotions alone. She and her brother never spoke about it.

This happens in more families than we think. One response would be to keep brothers and sisters apart, and to always be on the lookout for suspicious behaviour in adolescent boys. This would not be healthy. What happened to Julie and her brother was part of a larger family dynamic. As in the story of John and David, we see children with unmet emotional needs who are left to their own devices in managing powerful feelings. Julie said of her family, "We never talk about anything. We live as if we're normal." There are several very important insights to be gained from this observation. The first is the *no-talk rule* followed in every dysfunctional family. There are some things many families just don't talk about. Sex is usually one of them. But just plain feelings can be included in this prohibited zone. In an emotionally healthy family, all feelings are allowed and all feelings are talked about. The second is the phenomenon of hiding behind *normal.* Dysfunctional families often take refuge in conformity. We live in a society that rivals the Victorian period for its enforcement of strict social standards. We have a word for it that the Victorians would never have dreamed of — *cool.* There is a cool way to do everything. There is a cool version of every product. Our job as good consumers is to buy and display as many of these cool behaviours and products as possible. This is how we gain social acceptance and social status. It is also the façade behind which we can hide what's really going on. Dysfunctional families can camouflage themselves in cool — or its synonym, normal.

Inter-sibling abuse is not reported because we are taught from a very early age that our most profound loyalty is to our family. This is a double-edged sword. Sometimes our loyalty to our family overrides our loyalty to ourselves and our right to a full life. As Julie once said of her childhood self, "I killed who she could have been." She told no one in her family out of a sense of loyalty and a feeling of love for her brother. These realities cannot be ignored.

What is the standard protocol for dealing with these situations in our culture? They must be reported to the authorities — usually meaning Children's Aid or the police. At this point the blunt instruments of judicial proceedings come to turn the child's world upside down. The effects of reporting can be as traumatizing as the events themselves. The perpetrator is punished, shamed, and humiliated. The victim can be re-victimized by the process of reporting the details of the abuse and then seeing her brother or father dragged to the public pillory. The family is torn apart. Careers are ruined. Financial security ends. Does this mean one should not tell? Of course not. As inadequate as some of our procedures may be, they are still preferable to a continuation of the abuse or a denial of past abuse, but are our current protocols the best we can do? As an enlightened, humane society, can we do nothing better for the victim? Can we do nothing better for the perpetrator, whose behaviour reveals a deep wound in his own psyche? Would more children and adults report abuse if they felt the perpetrator would get some kind of help? Victims are often such compassionate people that they choose to suffer themselves rather than bring suffering on another. Restorative justice, which I talked about earlier, must become the common practice in sexual abuse cases. As quoted earlier, it is "an approach that views crime and conflict principally as harm done to people and relationships." No crime fits this criterion more than sexual abuse.

Males far outnumber females as perpetrators of sexual abuse. We must look more deeply into this fact and ask ourselves why this is the case. What is it about the way we raise and socialize boys that leads to these statistics? Males are not natural-born predators, abusers, or rapists. For them to become such things, something must go wrong in their emotional development. This is why the topic of this book is so important. When we raise emotionally healthy boys, we deal directly with the social problems that plague us.

How to Prevent Child Sexual Abuse

Child sexual abuse does not come from a man in a trench coat hiding in the bushes. It is a by-product of our often confused human nature, of our disconnected and stressed lives. It is a by-product of our culture where unhealthy depictions of sex permeate all aspects of life and affect the minds of children and adults in unnatural ways. Ironically, at the same time that we are saturated in sexual images and language, we also live in a sexually repressive culture where natural needs, curiosities, and impulses get pushed underground only to come out in other ways. We are a neurotic society when it comes to sex. We live under a terrible conflict between what we really want — love, connection, and mutual respect — and what we are told we should want — sex, power, control, and pleasure with no regard for consequences. Children who live in a warm, loving, respectful environment where their physical and emotional needs are met with openness and respect do not seek to have these needs met elsewhere (either as victims or perpetrators). We need to practise and teach three things:

1. Body Awareness

When we talk about the physical needs of children, we are not just talking about food, clothing, and shelter. We are talking about touch and body awareness — awareness of one's own body and the bodies of others. We are talking about sensual experience as a positive and powerful thing to be promoted and celebrated. We are talking about pleasure in all its simple and beautiful forms. We are our bodies. We are not disembodied minds whose job it is to monitor, control, and *use* the body like some kind of machine. The root word of *abuse* is *use,* and in any kind of abuse, that is the essential problem: someone uses the body as though it was some kind of object.

2. Empathy

Empathy is the ability to understand and share the feelings of another person. We understand their feelings precisely because we share them. "We are the same. What you feel is just as valid as what I feel." We learn empathy when we learn to have our feelings fully and then recognize these same feelings in others. We abuse ourselves and each other when we repress our own feelings and deny them in others.

3. Boundaries

To respect the value of another person implies respecting the boundaries between us. "You are not me, and I am not you. I can control myself, but I cannot control you." Boundaries can be physical, psychological, or emotional. It is easy to see the violation of physical boundaries. "Don't hit." It is harder to see the violation of psychological boundaries. "Do what you're told." And it is perhaps hardest to see where emotional boundaries lie. "What? Don't you love me?"

Conclusion
A Boy's Inner Monologue

The day I wrote the last few pages of this book, I received two e-mails. One was from the mother of an eleven-year-old boy, and the other from the grandmother of a ten-year-old boy. Both were reports about their boys hitting other kids at school and getting in trouble for it. I know both of these boys very well. Without going into all the details of their case histories, I know they both have an overpowering need to be loved, and they do not get enough — from their parents, their extended families, and the adult caregivers in their lives. This is why they hit. These boys are always being managed, controlled, and given consequences, with the occasional dose of syrupy praise, but they are not loved enough. They are not seen and listened to and accepted for who they are. There is always an undertone that there is something wrong with them. "Stewart had a good week." "Stewart was good today." These comments imply a flip side message: we expect Stewart to be bad.

If a boy is given love, anger and fear will fall away. We are good at disciplining our boys, we are good at controlling them, and we are good at imposing consequences for their behaviour. We are not as good at loving them unconditionally, at giving them what they need. As a consequence for hitting, Stewart had his iPad taken away. When he cried, "No one loves me!" his grandmother replied, "It's because we love you that we cannot let you behave badly." This makes no sense in the mind of a child.

The four strongest and most important emotions in boys' lives are anger, fear, love, and trust. They are distinct forces in a boy's psyche, but they also have an intimate connection with each other. Anger results from one of two things: a need not met or an expectation not realized. Here we can jump immediately to love. The most profound need of every boy, indeed every child, is love. By love I mean unconditional positive regard. A child needs to know that they are loved for themselves, not for what they do but for who they are. This love is unconditional. They have value. When a child does not feel this most basic affirmation, they become angry. This anger may not express itself overtly as hitting or yelling or throwing a temper tantrum. It can also express itself as withdrawal, which is a form of self-protection. His inner monologue goes something like this:

I have a need for love. I cannot fill it myself. I am dependent on others to fill it. I cannot control this. I cannot always depend upon those I love to love me back. This makes me vulnerable. I am angry about that, and I am afraid it will happen (again). As I go on in life, it does happen again, and I withdraw more. I will protect myself from these unpleasant feelings. I will withdraw my love from others.

As a teenager, I want more power and control over my life, but I find I am still dependent on others. I want to move beyond the love bond I have with my mother, father, and siblings to friends and eventually a girlfriend. I am afraid of getting hurt, and I am angry that I cannot control all of this. I get angry when I do get hurt, by which I mean my need gets exposed. I am revealed for who I am — a vulnerable boy wanting love. I withdraw.

As a man, I would seem to have more power and control over my life. I still need love, but I still must depend on others to give it to me. I am angry that I cannot control this, and I am afraid it will not come or that once given it will be taken away. I fear what I can't control. I become angry when I cannot control things. I fear my need for love. I am angry about my need for love. I will close myself off. That way I can stay in control. That way I will never be hurt.

The fourth emotion is more like an ability than a feeling. Trust. *I need to know that I can trust at least one person in this world.* Trust in what? *Trust that you will not hurt me, that you will be kind to me. The only way I can feel this trust is when your love for me stays there — no matter how I act. You love me.*

Boys and men want nothing more than to love and be loved. Out of anger and fear, they often end up cutting themselves off from the thing they need most. If we can break through these two negative emotions and establish trust, we will find a vulnerable boy or a vulnerable man who needs and wants our love.

About the Author

Jane Jacobs was a journalist who became a leading authority on urban planning. When she was asked about her training, she replied that it came from sitting on her front porch in Greenwich Village, New York, and watching what was happening to the city around her. For thirty years, my front porch was my classroom, and for another ten years it was my counselling room. I have no formal training in psychology or pediatrics, but I have worked closely with thousands of boys over the course of my career as a teacher and mentor. I have listened to countless boys' stories, I have given a lot of thought to my own story, and I raised three boys.

I was born in 1959 and came to consciousness in the late 1960s, a time when the whole world seemed to be exploding into something new. When the dust began to settle, the group that came out of it best seemed to be women. They had totally redefined their place in the world and were permitted new ways of being. Nothing like this happened for men and boys.

I did not fit the stereotype for my gender. I was a highly sensitive boy growing up in small-town Ontario where hockey was the main socially sanctioned activity for self-definition and self-presentation. I faked an interest in hockey. My loves were writing and drawing, which I did in secret. I knew what it was to live in fear of being teased. I learned to hide, to camouflage, to deny. Like many boys, I put parts of myself away. I had a complex relationship with my mother that veered between intense attachment and hostile separation. My father was a mysterious, distant enigma scarred by death, alcoholism, and war. I loved them both intensely. I liked being a boy. I spent most of my time outside in a maple tree beside our house. I liked my boy energy, but, as I grew up, I began to feel the limits put on it.

As an adult, psychoanalysis and psychotherapy taught me to accept my unique nature, and the women's movement showed that it was possible to change society. I became the father of three boys with few reference points on how to do this. Over time, I came to specialize in working with boys to affirm their unique natures and their male energy — all beautiful, powerful, and mysterious. Their emotional health is our hope. I am particularly drawn to those boys who do not fit in — round pegs trying to fit into square holes. Whether it's problems with paying attention at school, language processing, sensory processing, anxiety, or high sensitivity, I remember how these things felt.

After all my years of working with kids, of reflection, and of research, and now that my own children have grown up and moved away, I have come to the conclusion that every child needs three things:

- To be seen for who they really are
- To be listened to no matter what they say
- To be touched with nurturing affection

As a society, we are now on the verge of a complete redefinition of what it means to be male. Men must change or be left behind. They have no choice. This will not mean abandoning male energy. It will mean embracing it in all its complexity rather than keeping it in the narrow box into which it has always been crammed. We need men with empathy to assume leadership in the project of raising emotionally healthy boys. We need men who will expand the definition of what it means to be male in their own lives. We need men who will tell their truth.

Bibliography

Abrams, Jeremiah, ed. *Reclaiming the Inner Child*. Los Angeles: Jeremy Tarcher, 1990.

Adams, Kenneth. *Silently Seduced: When Parents Make Their Children Partners*. Deerfield Beach, FL: Health Communications, 1991.

American Psychiatric Association. *Diagnostic and Statistical Manual of Mental Disorders DSM-5*. Arlington, VA: American Psychiatric Publishing, 2013.

Aron, Elaine. *The Highly Sensitive Child*. New York: Harmony Books, 2002.

____. *The Highly Sensitive Person*. New York: Harmony Books, 1997.

Aristotle. *Poetics*. Toronto: Oxford University Press, 2013.

Axline, Virginia Mae. *Play Therapy: The Inner Dynamics of Childhood*. Hesperides Press, 2011.

Ayres, Jean. *Sensory Integration and the Child*. Torrance, CA: WPS Publishing, 2005.

Barkley, Russell A. and Christine Benton. *Your Defiant Child*. New York: Guilford Press, 2013.

____. *Your Defiant Teen*. New York: Guilford Press, 2013.

Baron-Cohen, Simon. *The Essential Difference: Male and Female Brains and the Truth About Autism*. Toronto: Penguin Books, 2012.

Beck, Judith. *Cognitive Therapy: Basics and Beyond*. New York: The Guilford Press, 1995.

Bettelheim, Bruno. *A Good Enough Parent*. London: Pan Books, 1988.

Blake, William. *The Complete Poetry & Prose of William Blake*. New York: Anchor Books, 1997.

Bly, Robert. *Iron John: A Book About Men*. New York: Vintage Books, 1992.

Brizendine, Louann. *The Female Brain*. New York: Harmony Books, 2007.

___. *The Male Brain*. New York: Harmony Books, 2011.

Cain, Susan. *Quiet: The Power of Introverts in a World that Can't Stop Talking*. New York: Broadway Books, 2013.

Campbell, Joseph. *The Power of Myth*. New York: Anchor Books, 1991.

Carnes, Patrick. *Out of the Shadows: Understanding Sexual Addiction*. Center City, MN: Hazelden, 2001.

Coloroso, Barbara. *Kids Are Worth It: Raising Resilient Responsible Compassionate Kids*. Toronto: Penguin Canada, 2010.

Corneau, Guy. *Absent Fathers, Lost Sons: The Search for Masculine Identity*. Boston: Shambhala, 1991.

Diamond, Jed. *The Irritable Male Syndrome: Understanding and Managing the 4 Key Causes of Depression and Aggression*. Emmaus, PA: Rodale Books, 2004.

Dweck, Carol. *Mindset: The New Psychology of Success*. New York: Ballantine Books, 2007.

Faber, Adele and Elaine Mazlish. *How To Talk So Kids Will Listen and Listen So Kids Will Talk*. New York: Scribner, 2012.

___. *Siblings Without Rivalry*. New York: Norton, 2012.

Fox, Matthew. *Original Blessing*. New York: Tarcher/Putnam, 2000.

Frankl, Viktor. *Man's Search for Meaning*. Boston: Beacon Press, 2006.

Friedberg, Robert and Jessica McClure. *Clinical Practice of Cognitive Therapy with Children and Adolescents: The Nuts and Bolts*. New York: The Guilford Press, 2002.

Furth, Gregg. *The Secret World of Drawings: A Jungian Approach to Healing Through Art*. Toronto: Inner City Books, 2002.

Gibson, Joel. "Sexless in the City: A Gender Revolution." *The Syndney Morning Herald*. March 12, 2010.

Glasser, William. *Positive Addiction*. New York: Harper Collins, 2010.

Granic, Isabela, Adam Lobel, and Rutger Engels. "The Benefits of Playing Video Games." *American Psychologist*. January 2014.

Grubman-Black, Stephen. *Broken Boys/Mending Men: Recovery from Childhood Sexual Abuse*. Blue Ridge Summit, PA: Tab Books, 1990.

Gurian, Michael. *Boys and Girls Learn Differently*. New York: Jossey-Boss, 2010.

___. *The Wonder of Boys*. New York: Tarcher, 2006.

Hallowell, Edward and John Ratey. *Delivered From Distraction*. New York: Ballantine Books, 2005.

Hollis, James. *The Middle Passage: From Misery to Meaning in Midlife*. Toronto: Inner City Books, 1993.

___. *Swamplands of the Soul: New Life in Dismal Places*. Toronto: Inner City Books, 1996.

___. *Under Saturn's Shadow: The Wounding and Healing of Men*. Toronto: Inner City Books, 1994.

Hui, Ann. "Canadian Teens Lead Developed World in Cannabis Use: Unicef Report." *The Globe and Mail*. April 15, 2013.

Jung, Carl Gustav. *The Archetypes and the Collective Unconscious*. Trans. R.F.C. Hull. Princeton: Princeton University Press, 1990.

Kranowitz, Carol. *The Out-of-Sync Child*. New York: Perigee Trade, 2005.

Levant, Ronald. *Masculinity Reconstructed*. New York: Plume, 1996.

Levy, Ariel. *Female Chauvinist Pigs: Women and the Rise of Raunch Culture*. New York: Free Press, 2006.

Lew, Mike. *Victims No Longer: The Classic Guide for Men Recovering from Sexual Child Abuse*. New York: Quill, 2004.

Louv, Richard. *Last Child in the Woods: Saving Our Children From Nature-Deficit Disorder*. New York: Algonquin Books, 2008.

Love, Patricia. *The Emotional Incest Syndrome: What to do When a Parent's Love Rules Your Life*. Toronto: Bantam, 1991.

Lowen, Alexander. *Narcissism: Denial of the True Self*. New York: Touchstone, 1985.

Maltz, Maxwell. *Psycho-Cybernetics*. New York: Pocket Books, 1989.

Maté, Gabor. *In the Realm of Hungry Ghosts: Close Encounters with Addiction.* Toronto: Vintage Canada, 2009.

___. *Scattered Minds: The Origins and Healing of Attention Deficit Disorder.* Toronto: Vintage Canada, 2000.

Miller, Alice. *The Drama of the Gifted Child: The Search for the True Self.* New York: Basic Books,1996.

___. *For Your Own Good: Hidden Cruelty in Child-Rearing and the Roots of Violence.* New York: Farrar, Straus and Giroux, 2002.

___. *Thou Shalt Not Be Aware: Society's Betrayal of the Child.* New York: Farrar, Straus and Giroux, 1998.

___. *The Untouched Key: Tracing Childhood Trauma in Creativity and Destructiveness.* New York: Anchor Books, 1991.

Miller, Arthur. *Death of a Salesman.* Toronto: Penguin Books, 1976.

Monick, Eugene. *Castration and Male Rage: The Phallic Wound.* Toronto: Inner City Books, 1991.

___. *Phallos: Sacred Image of Masculinity.* Toronto: Inner City Books, 1987.

Neill, A.S. *Summerhill School: A New View of Childhood.* New York: St. Martin's Griffin, 1995.

Neufeld, Gordon and Gabor Maté. *Hold On to Your Kids: Why Parents Need to Matter More Than Peers.* Toronto: Vintage Canada, 2013.

Nhat Han, Thich. *Reconciliation: Healing the Inner Child.* Berkeley, CA: Parallax Press, 2010.

Owens, Eric, Richard Behun, Jill Manning, and Rory Reid. "The Impact of Internet Pornography on Adolescents: A Review of the Research." *Sexual Addiction & Compulsivity*, 19: 99–122, 2012.

Palmer, Parker. *The Courage to Teach.* New York: Jossey-Bass, 2007.

___. *Let Your Life Speak.* New York: Jossey-Bass, 1999.

Paul, Pamela. *Pornified: How Pornography Is Damaging Our Lives, Our Relationships, and Our Families.* New York: St. Martin's Griffin, 2006.

Pellis, Sergio M. and Vivien C. Pellis. "The Function of Play in the Development of the Social Brain." *American Journal of Play.* Winter. 2010.

____. "Play-Fighting During Early Childhood and its Role in Preventing Later Chronic Aggression." *Encyclopedia of Early Child Development: Aggression.* 2012.

Pollack, William. *Real Boys.* New York: Holt Paperbacks, 1999.

Real, Terrence. *I Don't Want to Talk About It: Overcoming the Secret Legacy of Male Depression.* Toronto: Scribner, 1997.

Reist, Michael. *The Dysfunctional School: Uncomfortable Truths and Awkward Insights on School, Learning and Teaching.* Philadelphia: XLibris Publishing, 2007.

____. *Raising Boys in a New Kind of World.* Toronto: Dundurn, 2011.

____. *What Every Parent Should Know About School.* Toronto: Dundurn, 2013.

Rogers, Carl. *On Becoming a Person: A Therapist's View of Psychotherapy.* London: Constable and Robinson, 2004.

Rohr, Richard. *The Eight Core Principles.* Cincinnati: Franciscan Media, 2013.

Rosenthal, Robert. *Pygmalion in the Classroom: Teacher Expectation and Pupils' Intellectual Development.* New York: Henry Holt & Company, Inc., 1968.

Sax, Leonard. *Boys Adrift.* New York: Basic Books, 2009.

____. *Why Gender Matters.* New York: Harmony, 2006.

Schein, Edgar. *Organizational Culture and Leadership.* Etobicoke, ON: Jossey-Bass, 2010.

Schwartz-Salant, Nathan. *Narcissism and Character Transformation: The Psychology of Narcissistic Character Disorders.* Toronto: Inner City Books, 1982.

Shengold, Leonard. *Soul Murder: The Effects of Childhood Abuse and Deprivation.* New York: Fawcett Columbine, 1989.

____. *Soul Murder Revisted: Thoughts About Therapy, Hate, Love, and Memory.* New Haven, CT: Yale University Press, 1999.

Sonkin, Daniel. *Wounded Boys, Heroic Men: A Man's Guide to Recovering from Child Abuse.* Holbrook, MA: Adams Media Corporation, 1998.

Steinem, Gloria. Interview with Eleanor Wachtel, Writers and Company. CBC Radio, 2001.

Strauch, Barbara. *The Primal Teen.* New York: Anchor Books, 2004.

Thomas, Alexander and Stella Chess. *Temperament in Clinical Practice*. New York: The Guilford Press, 1986.

Thoreau, Henry David. *Walden and Other Writings*. New York: Bantam, 1977.

Whitfield, Charles. *Healing the Child Within: Discovery and Recovery for Adult Children of Dysfunctional Families*. Deerbeach, FL: Health Communications, 1989.

Wilson, Edward O. *Biophilia*. Cambridge: Harvard University Press, 1986.

Index

Also by Michael Reist

Raising Boys in a New Kind of World

From video games to the Internet, technology is having a profound effect on today's boys. Author Michael Reist writes from the front lines. As a classroom teacher for more than thirty years and the father of three boys, he is in an ideal position to provide practical advice on how to communicate with boys and how to identify their problems.

Available at your favourite bookseller

 DUNDURN

VISIT US AT
Dundurn.com
@dundurnpress
Facebook.com/dundurnpress
Pinterest.com/dundurnpress